THE NEXT NIGHTMARE

THE NEXT NIGHTMARE

How Political Correctness Will Destroy America

Peter Feaman

Author of **Wake Up, America!**

Foreword by Congressman Allen West

The Next Nightmare © 2012 Peter Feaman

Published in Nashville, Tennessee by Dunham Books. For information regarding special sales or licensing, please contact the publisher:
Dunham Books
63 Music Square East
Nashville, Tennessee 37203
www.dunhamgroupinc.com

Trade Paperback ISBN: 978-0-9839-9067-3
Ebook ISBN: 978-0-9839-9068-0

Printed in the United States of America

Dedicated to
My children and my children's children

Acknowledgements

To Synesio, who first inspired me to do this. To the Boca Raton Central Rotary Club, Bob and John, who inspired me along the way. To Maryanne, Linda and Barbara, for their tireless efforts.

To my wife Sally, Ike, Doug … and Uncle Bert.

Table of Contents

Foreword

Osama bin Laden is dead but his ideology of hate lives on.

In service to my country, I have fought, first hand, the ideology of Islamic totalitarianism, and while all Muslims are not Islamic totalitarians in the same way that all Germans were not Nazis in the 1930's and 40's, we cannot let political correctness blind us to certain realities: namely, that there is a percentage of Muslims, both in the United States and abroad, who actively seek the destruction of America.

Unfortunately, our mainstream media and many of our political leaders want to understand Islam as we would all like it to be, peaceful and tolerant. However, this is not how millions of devout Muslims understand Islam.

That is why books such as the one you are about to read are so important. Peter Feaman has written a book which is easy to digest and clearly defines the enemy we face. The first goal in any successful military campaign is to know your enemy. *The Next Nightmare* accomplishes that goal of clearly defining our enemy.

What prevents us from knowing our enemy is not just a failure of our leaders. It is also blindness caused by political correctness. When tolerance becomes a one-way street, it leads to cultural suicide. *The Next Nightmare* successfully chronicles how political correctness will destroy our great Republic unless we are willing to identify our enemy and have the courage to speak out. Peter Feaman identifies our enemy and lays out a framework for our survival in this compelling work.

Bravo, Zulu! A must-read for all concerned Americans.

—Congressman Allen West

Preface

Bin Laden's life is over but the War on Terror lives on. As Americans rejoiced, and rightly so, Islamic Supremacists worldwide continued to scheme, plan and plot, undeterred in their quest to destroy the West.

For all of his influence in the Middle East, Bin Laden was just one head of a multi-headed snake. This book is a plea to all Americans of all religions and backgrounds reminding them that the fight has not ended and informing them that the fight did not begin when most Americans thought it did. This is also an urging to all Muslims who are people of real peace; to Muslims who would like to peacefully co-exist in the same country and society with non-Muslims to speak out and join in the call to reform Islam, renouncing those that espouse Islamic supremacy and rejecting those that endorse the murder and violence that such hatred incites.

Tolerance is a <u>two</u>-way street. Muslims here in America should respect the customs, practices and traditions Americans have adopted and developed during two centuries of this grand experiment in freedom that we call the United States and what oppressed people the world over call the land of opportunity. We enjoy the freedom to criticize some parts of the Muslim religion that contradict our traditional notions of the sanctity of human life, the equality of opportunity for men *and* women, and the notion that we are <u>all</u> "endowed by (our) Creator with certain unalienable Rights, (including) Life, Liberty and the pursuit of Happiness."

For those who fear that books such as this will foster racism and bigotry, I suggest that such sentiment underestimates the fundamental goodness of the American people. Any Muslim who joins in the call for the <u>reformation</u> of Islam will receive the applause and welcome they deserve.

A Warning

By the afternoon of September 11, 2001, Americans everywhere learned the name of Osama bin Laden, who was identified as the mastermind of the horrific murders that occurred that awful morning. National focus zeroed in on his apprehension. We have since learned that bin Laden's demise, tremendous as it was, failed to end the terror or the threat to freedom the world faces.

There is a monster on the loose about which neither the mainstream press, the Obama Administration or Congress will adequately inform us. It's been called *Islamofascism*, *Radical Islam, Islamic Fundamentalism, Islamism or Sharia Islam*. Whatever one names it, it is an ideology of hate that, in just a few decades, has killed tens of thousands around the globe. It threatens all Americans today.

It is killing hundreds of thousands in Ethiopia, Nigeria, Somalia, Kenya, Congo, the Sudan (the world watches as South Sudan is born but will ethnic cleansing by Islamists continue?), Malaysia, Indonesia, Thailand and the Philippines. Its death toll has spread across Afghanistan, Pakistan, Iraq, Libya, Yemen, Russia, Chechnya, Tajikistan, Kosovo, Bosnia, Ukraine, Turkey, Jordan, Lebanon, the new "democracy" in Egypt, and benefits from state sponsorship in Iran.

In Europe, scores were killed in train bombings in Spain, train and bus bombings in London and riots in France. Islamic terrorists have struck from Brazil to Australia, India, Bali and Sweden. The hateful ideology could have claimed more lives in London, Glasgow, Fort Dix, JFK Airport, Manhattan and Germany but for good intelligence and police work. Grieving families in Fort Hood were not so lucky.

Virtually anywhere can host the next eruption of carnage. But this conflict also wages on battlegrounds few fully contemplate because they take place not in physical space but spheres of influence. In a war that's as nontraditional as the War on Terror, these are combat zones that we can ill afford to cede if our quest to defeat radical Islam stands a chance at success. This book will examine:

- Why our government and the news media are misinforming us about radical Islam.
- What was once called the War on Terror, itself an inaccurate label, was later euphemistically softened even more into the vague and bland "Overseas Contingency Operations."
- How the intents of our enemies are far more heinous than we're told. Their end game isn't to voice a concern against U.S. "imperialism" or force America out of the Middle East, or "free" the Palestinians, or gain "parity" with the Israelis or offer an alternative socio-economic-religious vision for global architects to consider. It is domination, pure and simple.
- How Europe, *as we know it*, will disappear in our lifetime without bold intervention.
- How "tolerance" is cultural suicide when it's a one-way street. And all of this will leave you asking yourself the most important questions of all:

Will the values of Judeo-Christianity Survive? Indeed, will the religions of Judaism and Christianity survive?

Affirmative answers on either largely rest with you. If you do not care how those questions are answered, stop reading. If those questions gnaw at your very core, read this book. Then tell a friend.

Chapter 1
Know Your Enemies

"It Is Said That If You Know Your Enemies And Know Yourself, You Will Not Be Imperilled In A Hundred Battles; If You Do Not Know Your Enemies But Do Know Yourself, You Will Win One And Lose One; If You Do Not Know Your Enemies Nor Yourself, You Will Be Imperilled In Every Single Battle." —*The Art of War* by Sun Tzu

Knowing our adversaries is not like it used to be. At the onset of the American Revolution, Paul Revere rode his horse through Boston warning the townsfolk "The British are coming!" The Bostonians looked into their harbor, saw the tall ships, the hoisted Union Jack and prepared accordingly.

When Peal Harbor was attacked, the enemy states were obvious. World War II came home for the United States, and our fathers and grandfathers took up arms to defeat the fascists of their generation.

World War IV[1]
Two generations after Pearl Harbor we are again in a war. And once again it is a war for the survival of Western Civilization. It is a war to keep the freedoms and prosperity which our Western Civilization has wrought. Over the top, you say? Such an observation might deserve dismissal as an overstatement to the casual observer until February, 2006. Then all the world and especially the West, saw how our fundamental freedoms that we take for granted (e.g. freedom of speech, freedom of the press, and freedom of religion) suffered direct attack.

Worldwide rioting mushroomed overnight after the publication of the so-called "offensive" cartoons published in a Danish newspaper. The cartoons depicted, among other things, a picture of Mohammed with a bomb for a turban. Unfortunately, media outlets throughout the world responded to the Muslim rioting with precisely the wrong message. They ceased publishing the "offensive" material, thereby validating the Muslim demand of censorship and the abolition of free speech. This was the first major instance of media self-censorship to abide Islamic sensitivities, a trend that hasn't waned.

In September 2006, it was a speech by Pope Benedict XVI that ignited global Muslim outrage once again. Some radical Muslims even declared a "Fatwa" against the Pope, granting the faithful Muslim permission to kill the Pope as an acceptable response to his *quotation of a fourteenth century Byzantine Emperor.* So, what did Pope Benedict actually say?

In an address at the University of Regensburg on September 17, 2006, Pope Benedict referred to a series of conversations (circa 1391) between the Byzantine Emperor, Manumel Paleologus II, and a Persian Muslim on the subject of Christianity and Islam. Pope Benedict was discussing "faith and reason" and why faith *and reason* go hand in hand. Based upon that premise, Pope Benedict discussed how the 14th Century Emperor "touches on the theme of Jihad, and why spreading the faith through violence is something unreasonable." Quoting Paleologus II, the Pope said, "Not to act in accordance with reason is contrary to God's nature...God is not pleased by blood ... (therefore) spreading the faith through violence is something unreasonable. Whoever would lead someone to faith needs the ability to speak well and to reason properly, without violence or threats...."

Two days later, on September 19, 2006, al Qaeda in Iraq warned Pope Benedict XVI that al Qaeda's "War against Christianity and the West will go on until Islam takes over the world...."

Simultaneously, Iran's President Ahmadinejad called for more protest over the Pope's remarks on Islam. As with other so-called "insults" to Islam, protests broke out, not just in the Middle East, but across the globe. In the Middle East, demonstrators carrying black flags burned an effigy of the Pope. Why? Because the Pope, while acknowledging *that* part of the Quran which states, "(T)here is no compulsion in religion" (Sura 2:256), also quoted Paleologus II when he said in 1391, "Show me just what Mohammed brought that was new, and there you will find things only evil and inhuman, such as his command to spread by the sword the faith he preached…."

And thus, the "Fatwa" was issued.

In 2007, Jihadists were foiled in attempts to blow up a car in London, blow up Glasgow Airport in Scotland and blow up an American military base in Germany. In fact, on September 5, 2007, the headline read "Germans foil 'massive' attack on U.S. citizens."

"They were planning massive attacks," German Federal Prosecutor Monika Harns declared. Three Muslim men had stockpiled more than 1,500 pounds of hydrogen peroxide, the same chemical used by the perpetrators of the 2005 attacks on London's transport system that killed 56 people in order to detonate a massive explosion. All three of the men had attended a jihadist training camp in Pakistan in 2006.

In early summer 2007, the "Fort Dix Six" were arrested before they could attack Fort Dix, New Jersey. Shortly thereafter, three different men were arrested before their plan to incinerate JFK airport could come to pass. In 2009, a massive plot to bomb New York City stadiums on the anniversary of 9-11was disrupted with numerous arrests. The Broadway car bomber almost blew up Times Square in 2010. One Muslim terrorist in the United States did succeed at Fort Hood, Texas and yet, no government official was willing to declare the obvious, – Instead, the Obama administration has labeled the massacre as "workplace violence." Political correctness in our military not only allowed a Muslim terrorist to murder Americans; it prevented our officials from even calling the murders by their proper name.

As we should have learned from dealing with Nazi-fascism, appeasement or capitulation to those who seek to repress others or their freedoms will only lead to more demands, more repression and increased fascism. Neville Chamberlain promised "peace in our time" after agreeing to Hitler's demands in 1939. The invasion of Poland that same year reminds us all that appeasement in the face of evil does not work. Contrast Chamberlain's "peace" policy with the words his successor employed to describe his own policy regarding England's commitment to confronting Nazism. "You ask, what is our Policy?" Winston Churchill said to the House of Commons on May 13, 1940, as a newly appointed Prime Minister, "I will say; 'It is to wage war, by sea, land and air, with all our might and with all the strength that God can give us: to wage war against a monstrous tyranny, never surpassed in the dark lamentable catalogue of human crime. That is our policy.' You ask, 'what is our aim? I can answer with one word: Victory—victory at all costs, victory in spite of all terror, victory however long and hard the road may be; for without victory there is no survival.'"

The truly grave danger is that the warning signs of this epic struggle for the survival of Western Civilization and the Judeo-Christian ethic continue to go ignored by our politicians and media elite. Amazingly, in a memo emailed on March 23, 2009 to Pentagon staff members, the Defense Department Office of Security Review noted: "This [Obama] Administration prefers to avoid using the terms 'Long War' or 'Global War on Terror.' Please use "Overseas Contingency Operation."[2]

What? Wake up America, please, before it's too late.

In order to survive as a nation, all Americans must awaken to the nature of this gathering evil. Unfortunately, because of political correctness, calculated influence and cowardice, our leaders are unwilling to identify our enemy.

How did we get to this point?

The Islamic Revolution in Iran in 1979 marked the beginning of what some have called, "World War IV."[3] (World War III being the struggle against, and conquest of, Communist supremacy led by the former Soviet Union.) On March 30 and 31, 1979, a popular vote in Iran established an Islamic Republic. The next day, April 1, 1979, Ayatollah Khomeini proclaimed that it was "the first day of God's government." He established himself as the "Grand Ayatollah" for life. He awarded himself the title of "Imam," the highest religious rank in the Shia sect of Islam.

A killing spree followed, eliminating all political opposition. Dozens of newspapers and magazines were shut down and universities shuttered for two years in order to "cleanse" them of Western influence.

Before the year was out, Khomeini denounced the U.S. government as the "Great Satan" and "an enemy of Islam." (This identification of the U.S. was proclaimed during the Carter presidency a president obviously not known for any militaristic or aggressive foreign policy toward Islam.) Khomeini accused the United States of standing as the font of all of the world's evil. Carter then allowed the occupation of the U.S. embassy, and the capturing and holding as hostages, 66 American citizens. That year (1979), St. Lucie County, Florida resident Robert Frazer was living in Saudi Arabia. A flyer was placed on his car windshield during the Iranian revolution. It was from **The Organization of the Islamic Revolution in the Arabian Peninsula**. The text is partially reprinted here:

> "To you, the killers of the people in the Far East countries, Vietnam, Korea and Japan… the killers of the people in the Southern America and the Middle America (*sic*)… the killers of the people in the Middle East, the people all over the Islamic countries are with the Iranians.
>
> The people in the Arabian Peninsula are sharing with the rest of the Muslim peoples their willing (sic) in establishing THE ISLAMIC GOVERNMENT OF THE WHOLE UNIVERSE…" (*Emphasis theirs*)

Mr. Frazer knows firsthand the sting of the Islamist. About 30 years later in December 2007, his grandson was killed in action on the streets of Iraq while serving his Country as a U.S. soldier.

Back in Iran, the embassy hostages were returned upon the inauguration of Ronald Reagan in 1981, but that did not prevent further killing by Islamic supremacists. The U.S. Marine barracks in Beirut, Lebanon was bombed in 1983 killing 241 Marines. Thereafter, Iranian Islamic became supremacy entangled in a protracted war with the secular government of Iraq for the balance of the 1980's. But after the cessation of hostilities, the decade of the 1990's arrived and radical Jihad turned its venom toward the West once again. The World Trade Center bombing in 1993 marked the first attack on U.S. soil in this present day war against the West by Islamists. Still, the act of war was treated as a criminal event rather than another battle in a global conflict between two civilizations holding polar opposite values. As a result, the radical Islamists grew emboldened. In 1996, two U.S. embassies in Africa suffered horrific bombings. U.S. embassies are by law, sovereign U. S. soil. Yet again, America took little action, treating the bombings as isolated criminal events.

In 2000, the U.S. Navy ship, the *U.S.S. Cole* was bombed, killing nineteen sailors and injuring 39 others. A few dozen sailors! And yet, we as a nation yawned. The Spanish-American War of 1898 began because of the sabotage of the *Maine* in Havana, Cuba harbor. Even though some historians debate the legitimacy of its origins, at least "Remember the *Maine!*" proved to be a cry that empowered and emboldened the nation. Teddy Roosevelt and his Rough Riders fought for a sense of purpose and righteousness. One-hundred years later, when the *U.S.S. Cole* was attacked, there was no collective moral outrage from the nation's executive leadership.

President Clinton had the opportunity to have Osama bin Laden extradited to the United States in 1998. Clinton, in conjunction with his National Security Advisor, Sandy Berger, let him slip away. Americans will never know what other foreign policy failures took place, as that chapter of history was whisked away from the judgment of a nation when Berger removed countless sensitive documents from the National Archives in advance of the 9-11 Commission's investigation into what caused the events of that terrible day. Where was the outrage over the willful destruction of historic documents supposedly held for safekeeping in our National Archives? Berger pleaded guilty to a misdemeanor and in a deal negotiated with the Justice Department, paid a $10,000 fine and had his national security clearance suspended for three years.[4] Save some circles of conservative commentators, little scorn was directed at Berger.

And then, in a sneak attack more deadly than Pearl Harbor, on September 11, 2001, more than 3,000 innocent people were killed as the World Trade Center in New York, the greatest symbol of vibrant capitalism in the western world, was destroyed. Simultaneously, the Pentagon was attacked, the central hub of the Department of Defense, another grisly "first" in American history.

As if those two targets weren't ostentatious enough, let's remember the planes few people care to recall. The courageous passengers on Flight 93 spared the White House from attack, but it was grossly underreported that two other planes were discovered harboring clandestine box cutters. A Delta flight set to depart Boston and another Delta flight leaving Atlanta for Brussels carried concealed razors like the ones used by Islamists against unarmed civilian flight attendants that fated day. The September 11 Commission cited Khalid Shaikh Mohammed who originally envisioned up to ten planes bastardized as bombs on 9-11. We know of four. Looks like it was at least six, but the aforementioned flights with cached razors never took off because air traffic was grounded.[5]

Contemplate for a moment the gravity and depravity of an attack even more wide scale than the original. Clearly, this act exceeds the scope of any "crime." In intents, it arguably dwarfs Pearl Harbor, as it could have crushed ours and by extension the world's economies, our military nerve center, our Capitol building, Congress, and the White House. This is so bold it's not even an act of war; it was an attempt to win a war in one fell swoop. It was a knock-out punch aimed at crippling America on every home front needed to launce a successful counterattack. Only the detonation of a nuclear bomb would have wreaked more damage and trauma.

America actually "woke up" that day. The United States took action and the fronts on the war against radical Islam shifted. Unfortunately, because of political correctness, election year politics and the failure of the mainstream press to tell the truth, it wasn't long before most Americans fell back to sleep.

How can Americans arise once again from their slumber? The first step in an effort to re-awaken the American people must be to specifically identify the enemy we face.

Defining the Enemy

The continuing problem of not properly defining our enemy was exacerbated immediately after "9-11" when the Bush Administration characterized the conflict, we now face as a "War on Terror." We are not fighting a "War on Terror" any more than if the World Trade Center and the Pentagon had been bombed by B-52s flying at 40,000 feet and we called the conflict, the "War on High Flying B-52s." Terror describes the method of attack, but not who attacked us or who we, the West, are at war *with*. Terrorism is caused by people—people with a certain ideology. The failure to identify the enemy has now been exacerbated by the Obama Administration. In renaming the present conflict we are in as an "Overseas Contingency Operation," the American people are even more confused or worse—disengaged.

So, who is the enemy we in the West face?

On February 18, 2006, Bridgette Gabriel delivered a speech at the Intelligence Summit in Washington DC. Ms. Gabriel is the founder of *www. americancongressfortruth.com*…. She correctly identified the enemy:

> The most important element of intelligence has to be understanding the mindset and intention of the enemy. The West has been wallowing in a state of ignorance and denial for thirty years, as Muslim extremists perpetuated evil against innocent victims in the name of Allah…. *America cannot effectively defend itself in this war unless and until the American people understand the nature of the enemy that we face.* We are fighting a powerful ideology that is capable of altering human basic instincts. An ideology that can turn a mother into a launching pad of death. A perfect example is a recently elected Hamas official in the Palestinian territories who raves in heavenly joy about sending her three sons to death and offering the ones who are still alive for the cause.[6]

The enemy that we face are radical Islamists, Islamic supremacists or Islamofascists. Chuck Colson, on his website, www.breakpoint.org, adopts the Islamofascist moniker as does *New York Times* best-selling author Mike Evans, plus many others. James Woolsey, former CIA director, calls them Islamic Nazis.

The mainstream media, government officials and universities caught in the cultural suicide web of political correctness resist those labels. Former President Bush, in speaking on the occasion of the fifth anniversary of the 9/11 murders, identified, for the first time, the enemy as "Islamic Fascists" for the first time. After the predictable expressions of outrage by Muslim leaders— particularly their powerful public relations lobby, the Council on American-

Islamic Relations (CAIR), Bush, mainstream media outlets and politicians abandoned the term, leaving the American people, once again, adrift in a sea of moral vagueness about who we are fighting and why. The new war moniker offered by the Obama Administration obscures the issue even more.

Fortunately, not everyone in positions of influence is so verbally hamstrung. Natan Sharansky, Newt Gingrich and Mike Evans, among others, cry out for moral clarity on the language. If our leaders, like former Senator Rick Santorum of Pennsylvania, Congresswoman Sue Myrick from North Carolina and South Florida Congressman Allen West, will continue to forcefully articulate *who* the enemy is and *why* fighting and defeating them is essential to our survival and widespread stability, enough Americans would rally around the cause of freedom and self-preservation to support an aggressive policy against radical Islam, both here and abroad.

Who are Islamofascists or Islamic Supremacists?

Islamic Supremacists are Muslim extremists who, driven by a totalitarian political/religious and social ideology believe, like communists and Nazis before them that their ideology is superior to all others and are willing to enslave or kill those who disagree. How would this be accomplished? Stealth jihad involves the institution of Sharia law in the courts. Sharia law—which we are told is representing Allah's will as revealed in the Quran and employed to govern all facets of a Muslim's behavior—often enshrines and legitimizes gross levels of disparity of justice and ruthlessness in "criminal" punishment. In some nations without a long history of freedom and democracy, Sharia law is instituted by force of arms and usually precipitated by great civil unrest and violent overthrow of the established order.

The deposing of the Shah of Iran is the most obvious example in contemporary history of how Sharia law's adoption inflicts drastic impacts. In Afghanistan, the Taliban takeover, after the vanquishing of the Russians, was barely registered in the West but led to the direst of consequences.

In countries where Muslims are not yet a majority or even a significant minority of the population, the process of imposition of Sharia law over the nations is much more subtle. And that includes America.

As some state legislatures move to outlaw Sharia law, Islam apologists rush to blunt its brutality. The Leftist online publication, Salon.com, conducted an interview with New Jersey attorney Abed Awad—also an adjunct faculty member of Rutgers Law School, about its application in U.S. courts. Awad claimed, a constitutional requirement "to regularly interpret and apply foreign law—including Islamic law—to everything from the recognition of foreign divorces and custody decrees to the validity of marriages, the enforcement of money judgments, probating an Islamic will and the damages element in a commercial dispute," he said. "Sharia is relevant in a U.S. court either as a foreign law or as a source of information to understand the expectations of the parties in a dispute."[7]

The article curiously spared little ink on Sharia law being cited to justify wife abuse and murder. Awad described the legislative attempts to ban Sharia law as, "a monumental waste of time."[8]

"The only explanation is that they appear to be driven by an agenda infused with hate, ignorance and Islam phobia intent on dehumanizing an entire religious community," Awad said. "That a dozen states are actively moving to adopt anti-Sharia laws demonstrates that this is part of a pattern. This is not haphazard. Someone—a group of people—is trying to turn this into a national issue. I believe it will become an election issue. Are you with the Sharia or with the U.S. Constitution? It is absurd."[9]

More absurd is the fact that political correctness is preventing politicians and policy-makers from identifying stealth Jihad as such so as not to offend Islamic moderates. This concern is clearly unnecessary. Since 2002, the United States has invaded, occupied and, by force of arms, overthrown two Muslim nations. Those Muslims who are susceptible to being offended by such actions are already offended by now.[10] Our leaders must publicly identify our enemy — Islamic Supremacists.

What is the ideology of an Islamic Supremacist?

Islamic supremacists believe in the power of the state to sponsor and impose the Islamic religious code known as Sharia on all of its citizens. Such a government is a "church-state" that contemplates no separation of church and state, and tolerates no freedom of thought, freedom of press, or freedom of religion. This is borne out by observing any Muslim demonstration that appears to spring up anywhere in the world over the slightest provocation. For example, most Americans have seen pictures of the signs of the demonstrators on the Internet, even if the mainstream media are afraid to publish them. They state such endearing slogans as, "Anyone who insults Islam must die," ... "Freedom Go To Hell," and "Europe, Your Next Holocaust Is Coming." This should leave no doubt to even radical leftists like Michael Moore that had George Bush been a Muslim, Michael Moore would have long since been beheaded.[11]

Fronts in the War for Islamic Supremacy

1. The Islamofascist War in Europe

The importance of Europe to our cultural survival cannot be overlooked. The train bombing in Spain in 2005 changed the results of its presidential election, and now Spain can no longer be trusted as an ally in the war against Islamic supremacists. The *militaristic* Islamofascist war in Europe is underway. Here are a few highlights:

- On November 2, 2004, on a street in Amsterdam, Theo Van Gogh, a descendent of the great Dutch painter, was bicycling to work. He had produced, directed and broadcast a film about Islamic violence against Islamic women. On that cold, grey European day, a Dutch-Moroccan Muslim shot Van Gogh off of his bicycle. As Van Gogh lay dying in the street, he pleaded for his life. The assassin responded by shooting him again, after which he slit Van Gogh's throat and stabbed a knife into his chest with a letter attached. The letter said, in part, "I surely know that you, Oh America, will be destroyed. I surely know that you, Oh Europe, will be destroyed. I surely know that you, Oh Holland, will be destroyed."[12]

- In Germany, Muslim students approved of Van Gogh's murder, saying, "If you insult Islam, you have to pay."[13] This reaction was not a surprise to those who have been observing German culture over the preceding 20 years. The seeds of this German reaction had been sewn years earlier. In 2002, a German constitutional court ruled that the German school system in Berlin must teach its Muslim students, who are the majority population in an elementary school, a_Muslim curriculum. After that ruling, a letter was written to the local newspaper: "Germany is an Islamic country. Islam is in the home, in schools. Germans will be outnumbered. We (Muslims) will say what we want, will live how we want. It's outrageous that Germans demand we speak their language. Our children will have our language, our laws, our culture." [14]

- On July 7, 2005, a succession of four coordinated suicide bombings rocked the United Kingdom, exploding in three locations on the London Underground and destroying a double-decker bus, killing 52 civilians and wounding 700 others.

- In the fall of 2005, French authorities confronted rioters throughout the country. Contrary to how the press reported it as "poor vs. rich," the riots were a Muslim community's uprising. Headlines in newspaper articles across the United States read: "French Fear Riots Could Fuel Discontent—Some Predict Movement to Islamic Jihad."[15] On New Year's Eve, 2006, France was still under Marshal Law.[16] In January 2008, Muslim riots erupted once again in the streets of France. The headlines read; "Clashes in Paris similar to '05 riots," and "French riots spread; youths shoot at cops." A senior police union official said the violence "… was worse than during three weeks of rioting that raged around French citied in 2005." The reports by the mainstream press were naïve at best, or purposefully misleading at worst. The Associated Press reported, "... anger still smolders in France's poor neighborhoods, where many Arabs, blacks and other minorities live largely isolated from the rest of society."[17] That story is misleading on two levels. While the communities may be, "Arabs, blacks and other minorities..." they all have one thing in common ... they are Muslim. It's the elephant in the room that nobody wants to see. Secondly, the "isolation" is mostly by the community leaders' *own* choosing and with the blessing of the political establishment. Tolerance and multiculturalism have created pockets of segregated Muslim communities. As a result, France has cordoned off *over 700* "no-go zones," where neither the Napoleonic Code nor police are welcome.

- The Associated Press wasn't the only news agency to omit uncomfortable realities. Fox News reportedly succumbed to journalistic compromise. It knuckled under to internal pressure from its part-owner, Saudi Price, Alwaleed bin Tala bin Abdul aziz. He claimed in a Dubai press conference that he personally called Fox News owner, Rupert Murdoch to complain about news coverage when Fox News called the upheaval "Muslim riots." "I picked up the phone and called Murdoch and said that I was speaking not as a shareholder, but as a viewer of Fox." He said, "I said that these are not Muslim riots, they are riots. Within a half an hour the description was changed from 'Muslim riots' to 'civil riots.'"[18]

- In March 2008, Osama bin Laden made two Internet broadcasts threatening Europe with *jihad*. Apparently, the republishing of the Danish cartoons and the release of a short film about radical Islam *Fitna*, by Dutch filmmaker and member of the Dutch Parliament Geert Wilders, has put Europe in the crosshairs of the Islamofascists. In 2009, Great Britain denied a visa to Mr. Wilders for fear of offending its Muslim citizens and he was later indicted by his own country for "hate speech" crimes. He has since been exonerated.

"Fitna" featured footage of Muslim protestors with placards reading, "God bless Hitler." Wilders compared the Quran to Mein Kampf and said it should be banned. Who did Dutch authorities side with? Dutch Prime Minister Jan Peter Balkenende said the film unfairly paired Islam and violence. The Dutch court stated "In a democratic system, hate speech is considered so serious that it is in the general interest to...draw a clear line."[19]

Europe is in the process of becoming an Islamic colony. The political establishment is terrified of offending its Muslim population. *"Eurabia— The Euro-Arab Axis"* by Bat Ye'or (2005), states: "In her forceful book, <u>La Forza della Ragione</u> (*The Force of Reason*), Oriana Fallaci ponders the steady Islamization of Europe noting "it was all there for years and we didn't see it." This "all there" relates to burning questions. Why have generations of Europeans been taught in universities to despise America and harbor an implacable hatred for Israel? Why has the European Union (EU) proposed a constitution that willingly renounces and even denies its Judeo-Christian roots? Has the 1930's—World War II alliance of Arab Jihad with European Nazis and fascists—been resurrected today?[20] The answer is yes. (For more details see Chapter 2.)

Its manifestation is unfolding in ugly ways that create a real quandary for anyone who values civil, tolerant societies. In one particularly blatant act of open harassment in 2011, supporters of the Muslim mayor for Towers Hamlets—a London suburb—stormed a council meeting. They taunted the Labour leader, Josh Peck, with animal noises and changes of "Unnatural acts!" They called the Conservative leader, Peter Golds, "Mrs. Golds and poofter."

Most disturbing was the police response—or utter lack thereof.

"If that happened in a football stadium, arrests would have taken place," said Golds. "I have complained, twice, to the police, and have heard nothing. A Labour colleague waits three hours at the police station before being told that nothing would be done. The police are afraid of being accused of Islamophobia." [21]

2. The Islamofascist War in the Far East

Considering how they kowtow to Islamic ridicule and intimidation against their government officials, one shudders to think what the London bobbies might do if faced with the kind of Muslim aggression exploding in the Orient. The following report appeared the day after Christmas, December 26, 2005, by the Associated Press concerning Indonesia: "Masked, black-clad and brandishing machetes, the attackers sprang from behind the screen of tall grass and pounced on the four Christian girls as they walked to school. Within seconds, three of the teenagers were beheaded—fresh victims of violence that has turned this Indonesian island into yet another front in the terrorist wars. Sulawesi is one of several islands in what some call Southeast Asia's Triangle of Terror, a region encompassing the insurgency-racked southern Philippines in the North and the Malacou Archipelago; itself a scene of sectarian conflict to the West and close by is heavily Muslim southern Thailand where a two-year insurgency has left more than 1,100 dead. Muslim Christian violence from 2000 to 2003 killed some 1,000 people in Sulawesi and attracted Muslim militants from across Indonesia, ... and even from the distant Middle East." [22]

The Far East, from Thailand to the Philippines, struggles daily with Islamofascist violence, yet the violence goes largely unreported in the mainstream media.

On December 12, 2007 an Indonesian court sentenced four "Islamic militants" to 19 years in prison for terrorist acts *including the beheadings of three Christian schoolgirls* and a deadly market bombing. Mohammad Basri, one of the three convicted, was also found guilty of shooting a priest and two students in 2004. It provides little comfort to say that at least they were convicted.

3. The Islamofascist War in Africa

Nigeria

In Nigeria, Muslim radicals have targeted mainly Christians but the violence has been widespread and deadly, largely unreported by the mainstream media.

Sudan

Slowly, world attention was increasingly drawn to the civil war in the Sudan which spilled over into Chad with much less fanfare. What has not been reported is the fact that the "Arab" insurgents are militant Islamofascists engaged in the systematic destruction of the Christian people of southern Sudan. Although the slaughter has been reported, it has not been reported as Muslims vs. Christians. In early 2011 the new nation of South Sudan was formed. Time will tell if the Islamic supremacists of Sudan will resume their ethnic cleansing.

In late 2007, a British schoolteacher, Gillian Gibbons, 54, was arrested for insulting Islam by naming a teddy bear Mohammed for her 7-year-old students. She was later sentenced to receive 40 lashes.

Somalia and Ethiopia

Pirates off these African countries' coast roam virtually free. February 2011 saw the capture of an oil tanker bound for the United States. Those ignorant of history are doomed to repeat it. The Barbary Coast pirates who threatened Atlantic trade routes during the presidency of Thomas Jefferson were also radical Islamists. Their hostility didn't merely interrupt trade routes; it included murdering and enslaving sailors and passengers. This prompted our nation's third president to send in the Marines. The war gave birth to the line in the Marine Corps Hymn "From the halls of Montezuma *to the shores of Tripoli*...." When U.S. Navy SEALS rescued the American merchant marine crewmembers from the clutches of Somali pirates, history in this region turned full circle.

4. The Islamofascist War in the Middle East

Iraq

This book offers no opinion on the pros and cons of the invasion of Iraq. Suffice it to say, however, that much of the violence there reveals a fundamental flaw of U.S. military thinking. The war planners did well in preparing for the *war*. They failed terribly in preparing for the *peace*. Why? They forgot the premise of this chapter. They did not know or understand the true enemy. The enemy in Iraq is not the "insurgents" as the press dubbed them. They are the same Islamic supremacists that cause and are causing death and destruction around the globe. The bitter internal struggle fought there, and fought today only with far less media interest, is a war between moderate Sunni Muslims and radical Shia Islamic Supremacists, largely from Iran. Understanding the enemy from the beginning might very well have brought about stabilization much more quickly.

Iran

The President of Iran, Mahmoud Ahmadinejad, states that he wishes to wipe Israel off the face of the map. In September 2006, addressing the U.N. General Assembly in New York, Ahmadinejad prayed for the Islamic messiah to usher in an era of world peace and the conversion of all peoples to Islam. The *unspoken* prayer, according to Muslim eschatology—the study of end times prophecy—was that the appearance of the Muslim messiah must be preceded by a *world-wide conflict* wherein the world is cleansed of all "infidels." Note: Any non-Muslim is an "infidel." So by praying for the coming of the Islamic messiah, Ahmadinejad is praying for a world war of Islam vs. the infidels unless the infidels succumb to coerced conversion. Even then, Islamic code condemns forced converts to a second-class status.

Ahmadinejad has become the spokesperson and world leader of the Shia Islamic Supremacists. We are in the process of witnessing Islamofascism transfer itself from a terrorist confederation, operating as a rogue non-state organization, into a government-led, state-sponsored terrorist war machine. (See Iraniumthemovie.org.) An Islamofascist militarized state, such as Iran, actively seeking nuclear weapons, reveals that the death of Osama bin Laden is only a small victory in the overall war on Islamofascism. The death of bin Laden no more ends the "War on Terror" or the "Overseas Contingency Operation" than capturing Mussolini would have ended World War II.

Ahmadinejad called Israel a "permanent threat" to the Middle East that will "soon" be liberated. He stated, "Like it or not, the Zionist regime is heading toward annihilation…. The Zionist regime is a rotten, dry tree that will be eliminated by *one storm.*" As Iran seeks nuclear capability, it's not hard to figure out what that "one storm" might be. Ahmadinejad has stated "Israel must be wiped off the map" and that "the existence of this (Israel) regime is a permanent threat to the Middle East. Its existence has harmed the dignity of Islamic nations."[23]

Further, what the mainstream media or our leaders in Washington have not discussed with any clarity is what Ahmadinejad has said about the United States. Ahmadinejad, in the same statement referenced above, called for "eliminating the United States from the world." He also called for backing terrorism against any Muslim country that made peace with Israel. Curious how this admission hasn't garnered more press interest. Now that Mubarak of Egypt has stepped down, is an Iran-style revolution coming to Egypt? The latest developments in Iran show that its government still defies the West and the U.N. by advancing its attempts to enrich uranium for "energy production." However, Iran sits one of the world's largest supply of oil, second only to that of Saudi Arabia. Iran also contains one of the world's largest reserves of natural gas. Can anyone seriously accept Iran's claims that it seeks nuclear capability for "peaceful" energy purposes as it attests? An oppressive regime that publicly bellows incessantly about wiping America and one of its most important democratic allies (Israel) off the face of the Earth bears a particularly high burden of proof when claiming peaceful intents for any of its endeavors—much less its "right" to go nuclear.

Territories Occupied by Palestinians

The election of Hamas in 2006 as the governing body of Palestine is one of the most stinging reminders of just how mercilessly the law of unintended consequences can render a verdict. The Bush Administration's desire and efforts to see democratic institutions flourish across the Middle East liberated untold millions from the rule of barbarous tyrants. But much of the ambition of Bush's foreign policy has operated on a delayed, time-release manner. It has manifested itself years later, in the 2011 "Arab Spring" in Egypt, Tunisia, Libya, Syria, and Yemen. The mechanics of the democratic process do not guarantee a democratic outcome. Granting Palestinians the right to vote—for Hamas—certainly falls within the law of unintended consequences. Consider what such a centrally located terror state sounds like. The following is a quote from Hamas leader Khaled Mash'al at a mosque in Damascus from February 2006: "Today the Arab and Islamic nation is rising and awakening and it will reach its peak, Allah willing. It will be victorious. It will link the present to the past. It will open the horizons of the future. It will regain the leadership of the world. Allah willing, the day is not far off... this victory which was clearly evident in the election, conveys a message to Israel, to America and to all the oppressors around the world: today you are fighting the Army of Allah. You are fighting against peoples for whom death for the sake of Allah and for the sake of honor and glory is preferable to life.

You are fighting a nation that does not tire, *even after 1,000 years of fighting.*... Before Israel dies, it must be humiliated and degraded." [24]

The crowd then shouts "Death to Israel, death to Israel, death to America."

On April 14, 2008 the *Fox News* headline read: "*Hamas Cleric Predicts 'Rome Will Be Conquered By Islam.'*" A prominent Muslim cleric, who is also a member of the Palestinian Parliament, openly declared "The capital of the Catholics, or the Crusader capital," would soon "be conquered by Islam."

The rhetoric is bad enough. But matters worsen when an authority no less than a U.S. president admonishes Israel to enter into negotiations with the Palestinian Authority while acknowledging its ties to Hamas, as President Obama did in a speech to the State Department on May 19, 2011.[25]

Afghanistan

On March 29, 2008, an arsonist set fire to a radio station in Kabul, Afghanistan for being un-Islamic. Its programming included shows on Islam, sports, news and music. The station had sixteen employees, including two female journalists. It was considered non-compliant with Sharia law and therefore worthy of destruction. One has to question whether we really have "liberated" Afghanistan—even ten years later. Apostasy is a capital crime. Afghanistan sentenced to death a prominent citizen for renouncing Islam in 2006. He has since sought and obtained asylum in Italy.

Saudi Arabia

In Saudi Arabia you will find no churches or synagogues. Full Sharia law is in effect. Women are second-class citizens. (That may be too kind of a characterization. As Amnesty International describes, discrimination against women isn't merely prevalent in Saudi society, in some cases it's "required by law.")[26]There is no freedom of the press, freedom of speech, or freedom of religion. For women, there is no freedom to drive.

Tunisia, Egypt and Lybia

Those countries have now deposed their leaders. It remains an open question as to whether Islamic supremacists will take their places.

It is obvious that neither our political leaders nor the mainstream press are connecting the dots. By stringing together into one paragraph the various quotes of Ahmadinejad and other Islamofascists around the world, one easily concludes there is an ongoing clarion call for the imposition of Islamic rule worldwide, by force of arms or otherwise. Even more clearly, a war *has* been declared against not only Israel and the United States, but the entire West. For the student of history, this is all too eerily similar to Germany in the 1920s and '30s. The strategy of a radical minority intimidating a non-radical majority is the same process that took place in Germany in the pre-World War II decades. Like the Nazis who intimidated moderate Germans, first into silence, then collaboration, and ultimately full support; so the moderate Muslim world is intimidated into silence and, in many quarters, full support of the radical Islamofascists and their terrorist activities. Societies that produce poor and disenfranchised Muslim youths in Europe and elsewhere form a perfect petri dish in which Islamofascists cultivate an ideology of hopeful hate that indoctrinates recruits into worldwide conflict where converting or ridding the world of infidels is necessary and honorable. How else could they accomplish their next goal—ushering in the global caliphate?

If there is one thing we should have learned from those dark years of pre-World War II Germany: when a head of state says that he wants to kill you, believe him and capture or kill him before it's too late. The killing of bin Laden is a helpful example even though his demise does not spell the end of Islamic aggression. Nevertheless, those ignorant of history are doomed to repeat it and the warning signs, despite our desire to live life in blissful ignorance, are all around us. We are still a nation at war. And we have a lot to lose.

Chapter Two

The Three Little Pigs and the Islamization of Europe
(Winston Churchill, where are you?)

Europe, as we know it, will cease to exist in twenty years time. It is already in extreme decline due to a demographic "perfect storm."

What is really going on in the land of our forefathers and the lands from which our laws, culture and heritage descended? The results are shocking. By no means should we consider them occurring in a vacuum.

The confluence of three events or trends persistent across today's in Europe is perpetuating the demise of a civilization that, for eight hundred years, led the planet in political, scientific and spiritual thought; a civilization that took the world from the Dark Ages to the post-modern era. A civilization that took the human race to its greatest longevity in life span, its lowest infant mortality rate and more advances in science, technology and the arts than the world has ever seen.

And yet, that great light of Europe is about to be extinguished.

Event No. 1: The Birth Dearth

The European twentieth century witnessed two wars so horrific, in two successive generations; that these conflicts alone might have caused the decline and fall of its civilization and culture.

America recovered from World War II as soldiers returned home and had babies (lots of them) sparking the "baby boom" generation. In Europe, however, although some repopulation occurred, no such demographic explosion took place. In American cities, homes and infrastructure escaped the devastation of World War II, and in 1946 Americans simply returned to work in a peacetime economy. In Europe, the people had to start, literally, from scratch. The re-builders faced destroyed farms and villages, decimated cities, ravaged infrastructure, and worse, no determined people bent on re-populating the continent.

Although Europeans rebuilt their infrastructure, there arose among them a parallel intellectual self-reexamination. The academic review soon turned cannibalistic. It resulted in an intellectual European self-recrimination, expanding to such an extent that a tremendous anti-Western stream of thought took root within the European academic elite. This philosophy of nihilism, no surprise, inhibited any significant post-war baby-boom generation in Europe. Its influence persists. For the last fifty years, Europeans have simply decided not to have children. These demographic events are pushing Europe into oblivion, while its academic and political elites accelerate the demise with their own brand of cultural suicide, multiculturalism.

Consider some demographic statistics:

A birth rate of 2.1 children per couple is needed for a population to merely maintain itself. However, the birthrates across much of Europe reveal a culture unwilling to reproduce in order to survive in the long term.

- In France, the birthrate is 1.8 children per couple. Because of immigration, one-third of all babies born in France are now of Muslim parents.
- In Belgium, the birthrate is now 1.2 and *fifty percent* of all babies born in Belgium today are of Muslim parents.
- In Germany, the birthrate is 1.3. In the next twenty years, Germany will lose one-third of its native population.
- In Spain, Italy and Russia it is even worse. In Italy the birthrate is 1.2, in Russia 1.17 and in Spain, an astounding 1.07.

Europe, as a whole, has a birthrate of 1.4. As a result, Europe will lose *one hundred twenty-eight million* (128,000,000) indigenous people by the year 2050. This demographic demise is worse even than the black plague that struck Europe in 1347.[27]

However, the loss of the European indigenous population *will be replaced.* They will be replaced by immigrants. And who will these immigrants be? Here is a look at who they have been.

Event No. 2: Muslim Immigration

The second event of this demographic perfect storm is Muslim immigration into Europe during the past sixty years.

In 1945, Europe launched the enormous undertaking of post-World War II reconstruction. The continent needed great numbers of "guest workers" in order to rebuild. For forty years they came by the hundreds of thousands from places like Turkey, Morocco and Tunisia. They were overwhelmingly Muslim.

The first Muslim immigrants came without their families. But things did not work out as expected by the European leaders who first conceived of the "guest worker" plan. The Muslim "guest" status soon changed. Wives followed the workers. The predictable result was, of course, children. The guest worker visas then turned into permanent visas. Then more children arrived, great numbers of them Muslims, but now, they were born in Europe as European citizens.

But *this* immigrant explosion was different from what we here in the United States experienced when our periods of great immigrations took place. Unlike the Irish, Italians, Jews from all over the world, Poles, Scandinavians, Koreans and Vietnamese, all of whom have assimilated and blended into a uniquely American culture, the Muslims in Europe did not, and are not, assimilating into the European fabric of society. In fact, it is just the opposite—they're outright rejecting it.[28]

In Berlin, young Muslim immigrant women have been murdered *by family members*—for, well, behaving like Germans. What German behavior is so offensive as to merit a death sentence to be carried out by members of their own families? The wearing of western style clothing and being caught alone with another single male merits death. This conduct so embarrasses and humiliates the Sharia compliant Muslim family that they permit brothers to slay their sisters. Multicultural tolerance has helped create a parallel segregated society in the heart of Europe.[29]

Europe would do well to imitate the American model of immigration as first espoused by Theodore Roosevelt in 1907:

> In the first place, we should insist that if the immigrant, who comes here in good faith, becomes an American and assimilates himself to us, he shall be treated on an exact equality with everyone else, for it is an outrage to discriminate against any such man because of creed, or birth place, or origin. But this is predicated upon the person's becoming in every facet an American and nothing but an American.... There can be no divided allegiance here. Any man who says he is an American, but something else also, isn't an American at all. We have room for but one flag, the American flag.... We have room for but one language here, and that is the English language ... and we have room for but one sole loyalty and that is a loyalty to the American people.[30]

But the Europeans have not adopted the American model. The European model of open borders and tolerance has led to accommodation. Accommodation then leads to acceptance of mores and values totally antithetical to Western norms. The imposition of Sharia law follows and soon, stealth jihad has subjugated a continent without a shot being fired.

As Europe becomes "more tolerant" and "more sensitive," the Muslims increase their demands for a separate culture and separate laws. For example, for twenty years, the Islamic Federation of Berlin struggled in the courts to secure Islamic religious instruction in public elementary schools. In 2001 they succeeded by using the judicial system in much the same way that the American Civil Liberties Union uses the judicial system in the United States to obtain by judicial fiat that which cannot be accomplished through the legislature. Based upon a German constitutional court ruling, today thousands of children in Berlin are taught by teachers hired by the Islamic Federation and paid with taxpayer money. Because of political correctness, instructors hold lessons in Turkish or Arabic, *behind closed doors*. [31]

In Belgium, Bishops permit North African—read Muslim—illegal immigrants who are threatened with deportation to seek sanctuary and to hold prayer services in historic and beautiful Brussels cathedrals. A German judge refuses the desperate plea of an abused Muslim woman for an expedited divorce because in the culture of Sharia Islam, it is permitted for a husband to beat his wife. In early 2008, the Archbishop of Canterbury urges Britons just to accept the coming of Sharia law in the United Kingdom. Taxi drivers in Norway refuse to carry blind passengers with seeing-eye dogs because dogs are deemed unclean animals in Islam.

American immigration policy makers should learn from this European experience. Today in America, the Roosevelt model of immigration has been lost. Unbridled immigration through the southern border of the United States results in demands by Mexican immigrants, both legal and illegal, for bilingualism and special concessions designed to show tolerance of the Mexican culture.

This is now being applied to Muslims in this country. The University of Michigan bends to the demands of its Muslim students for the installation of footbaths and the provision of prayer mats. In Dearborn, Michigan an exception is made to that city's noise ordinance to allow for the blaring of the Muslim call to prayer five times per day.

Event No. 3: The Rise Of Jihad Or Islamofascism

In and of itself, Muslim immigration would not pose a threat to western values and the West's concepts of freedom of speech, freedom of the press and freedom of religion were such immigrants encouraged to follow the Teddy Roosevelt model of immigrant attitudes. However, as we witness the worldwide rioting, murder and mayhem invoked in reaction to the publication of an editorial cartoon deemed offensive to Muslim dogma, or statements by the Pope (or anyone else for that matter) who dares to insult Islam, the danger assumes a frightening reality. Some of the placards displayed and chants recited during the riots that took place all over the world make the western concept of tolerance look like empty-headed nonsense:

"Behead Those Who Insult Islam."

"Europe, you will pay; extermination is on the way."

"Butcher those who mock Islam."

The signs warn Europeans of their own impending 9/11: "Europe: your 9/11 will come."[32]

This brand of Islamofascism *does* threaten Western ideals of freedom of the press, religion and speech. There is no constitutional right <u>not</u> to be offended by free speech.

Some of the highlights (or lowlights) of Jihad in Europe since 9/11:

1. March 11, 2004: Multiple train bombings in Spain, killing 191 people and injuring 1,460.

2. November 2, 2004: The murder of Theo Van Gogh in Holland by jihadist Mohammed Bouyeri.

3. July 7, 2005: Multiple subway and bus bombings in London killing 53 people and injuring nearly 700 others.

4. October, November 2005: The Muslim riots in France, reportedly affecting 274 towns, damaging 8,973 cars, injuring 126 police and firefighters, resulting in two deaths, sparking 2,888 arrests and causing more than 200 million Euros in damage.

5. The outrage of Islamofascists over the cartoon of Mohammad with a bomb for a turban, appearing in a Danish newspaper resulted in a slew of violent protests, riots and embassy attacks.

6. The vitriol of Islamofascists in reaction to Pope Benedict's speech intended to promote interfaith dialogue, where a Pakistani terror group ordered a fatwa against the Pope.

7. The foiled attempt in the summer of 2006 by Islamofascists to blow up transatlantic flights originating in London.

8. The June 2007 London and Glasgow Airport attempted and actual van bombings.

These events in Europe bring to the fore and crystallize the ongoing global clash of civilizations and, more specifically, the growing conflict in Europe. The violence is only a harbinger of things to come. The *jihad* declared by

Iranian President Ahmadinejad against Israel and the West and the *jihad* declared against Europe by Osama bin Laden in March 2008 is translated as "my struggle." In the German language, "my struggle" is translated into the words "Mien Kampf."

This is how it all started 80 years ago in Nazi Germany. The winds of war are blowing once again as freedom has come under attack. And now in Europe, their freedom of the press and freedom of speech are coming under direct attack by Islamic Jihad.

How should Europe have responded? How shall Europe respond?

Every newspaper in Europe and the Americas should have re-published the so-called offensive cartoons in order to reinforce the notion that freedom must not succumb to violence, threats or intimidation. Unfortunately, just the opposite was the case, as freedom retreated with each apology.

Why does an Islamized Europe threaten the United States?

Europe is a major power. In land mass Europe is larger than the United States and its population outnumbers that of America. As a colony of Islamofascism, Europe would pose a grave threat to the security and survival of <u>our</u> culture. Virulent anti-American policies emanating from Europe or "Eurabia" (an Islamisized Europe) would threaten our trade policies and our economy, as well as our allies and interests around the world.

Without Europe as a political partner, our ability to deal with the threat of a nuclear Iran is severely compromised. An Islamized Europe further isolates the United States in its attempts to halt the spread of Islamofascism, as much as a pro-communist Western Europe would have made it almost impossible to halt the spread of communism during the Cold War. For example, 20 years later, it is routinely acknowledged, perhaps begrudgingly by some, that the deployment of Pershing missiles to Western Europe by the United States in the 1980s raised the ante for Russia so much that the economic collapse of the United Soviet Socialist Republic was hastened, thereby accelerating the breakaway of the Eastern Block countries and the destruction of the Berlin Wall. The final result was the liberation of more than twenty million people, who for a generation lived under communist fascism.

More importantly, an impotent Europe has *already* harmed us. The 9/11 attacks were plotted in Hamburg, Germany. The individual assassins of the leaders of Afghanistan's Northern Alliance (the opposition to the Taliban) all carried Belgian passports. Zacarias Moussaoui, who in March 2006 was sentenced to life in prison in the United States for his part in the 9/11 attacks, was *born in France and educated in Britain.* The foiled attacks by Islamofascists in their attempts to blow up airliners en route from England to the United States was planned and almost carried out by Islamofascists based in England and continental Europe.

Economically speaking, as the United States does everything possible to work with the international community to rein in Iran's nuclear ambitions, France is clearly not our ally. France finds itself in the position of being Iran's largest creditor nation, so it is conflicted in its loyalties. Germany shows up as the largest lender to the countries of Syria and North Korea. As a result, America's struggle becomes that much more difficult when even our traditional Cold War allies are aligned against us in order to protect their own economic self-interest. This is an understandable aim for any nation, except when that economic interest hinges on the rationale of a terror-state that is panting after nuclear warheads and promising to obliterate the only democracy in its neighborhood.

What about Britain?

Unfortunately, Tony Blair and his unwavering support of the United States may have been the last breath of comfort from even our oldest and culturally closest ally. Blair has departed office. Meanwhile, at least two influential segments of British society hate the United States no less than if they had been educated in Mecca. Britain's traditionally leftist academics and trade unions on the one hand, and Britain's ever growing Muslim population on the other, are finding common ground in a common enemy, the U.S.. This bodes ill for England's continuing support of United States' policy in regard to Islamofascism. After the publication of the offensive cartoons that sparked Muslim riots worldwide, some of the most hateful demonstrations against the publications arose in England. Placards not shown to the American people by the mainstream media, being held by British citizens of Muslim descent, stated such confrontational slogans as, "Europe, your real holocaust is coming."

Britain's academics and intellectual crowd, like their counterparts in the United States (see Chapter 4) share the same anti-all-things-American sentiment. Unfortunately, this anti-Americanism is a much more virulent strain than that found in the United States. Note the words of British playwright, Harold Pinter (winner of the Nobel Prize for literature, no less) in 2002, *before* America's invasion of Iraq: "The U.S. administration is now a bloodthirsty wild animal. Bombs are its only vocabulary."[33] Well, thank goodness America's "vocabulary" spoke loud and clear: the leader of Al-Qaeda in Iraq, Al-Zachari, is no longer around to behead American journalists on TV, or anyone else who might disagree with his utopian vision of Muslim freedom and prosperity. In 2003 an opinion piece by Mr. Pinter appeared in London's *Daily Telegraph* entitled, not so subtly, "*I Loathe America.*" The op-ed piece began with "My Anti-Americanism has become almost uncontrollable..."[34] See also www.18doughtystreet.com.

The re-election of George W. Bush in 2004 sent folks like Pinter over the edge. The anti-American hate filtered into the orations of highly elected British public officials. Only one month after the British train and bus bombings in 2005, British MP George Galloway, whose record of Islamist-praising remarks demonstrates he is on a jihad of his own, said this: "It's not the Muslims who are terrorists. The biggest terrorists are Bush and Blair … but it is definitely not a clash of civilizations. Bush doesn't have any civilization."[35]

Does this awful rhetoric have an effect on the British populace? You bet it does. A February 2003 poll commissioned by Britain's TV Channel 4 revealed that a majority of Britons view the U.S. as the bigger threat to world peace rather than Iraq. [36] The British Teachers Union followed suit, passing resolutions condemning the United States and its foreign policy. When you consider this information in conjunction with the fact that more people in Britain attend weekly services at mosques than worship at the Church of England, you begin to get the picture. Has England forgotten the failure of Neville Chamberlain's appeasement policy? Winston Churchill, where are you?

It comes down to this: Europeans of Judeo-Christian descents have lost sense of their cultural and historical past. The European people have lost their present identity and therefore, and most importantly, they have lost their vision for the future. A people without vision will perish. For a generation, academic elites in both Europe and the United States have denigrated Western culture and its values. Without a sense of the past, why look to the future? As a result, Islam has marched into that spiritual and cultural vacuum. What happens after that? Those tolerant of the intolerant will perish.

Is it too late for Europe? Read the re-telling of the childhood fairytale, "The Three Little Pigs." This updated version could be re-titled "The Three Euro Pigs."

The Three Pigs
(In a Form of Prose Meant for the Youngest of Readers)

Once upon a time there lived three little pigs. They lived alone in a great big beautiful old house. And inside the house of the three little pigs there were many beautiful pieces of art, sculpture and great works of literature.

Little pigs had been living in this great, big, beautiful old house for many, many years. Over the years, stories had been passed down from generation to generation about the Big Bad Wolf. The story was repeated from grandpig to little pig that many, many years ago, the Big Bad Wolf had come to huff and puff and blow the house down. As the old story was told, the Big Bad Wolf would come to the door and yell: "Open the door and let me in, or I'll huff and I'll puff, and I'll blow your house in!" And the little pigs were always taught to say "no, no, no, not by the hair of our chinny, chin, chins." This was so because little pigs were always told that there were *differences* between pigs and wolves. The main difference between the two was that the Big Bad Wolf liked to *eat* little pigs, even though pigs would never purposefully harm a wolf.

But, things had changed of late. When the three little pigs were younger and went to school, they were told that the Big Bad Wolf really wasn't so bad. They were told that the only reason the Big Bad Wolf ate little pigs was because in the past, many, many years ago, little pigs had been mean to the Big Bad W lf and killed wolves. The three little pigs were now being told that because the wolf hadn't eaten pigs in a long time, there was no longer a reason to fear the Big Bad Wolf. And the three little pigs were told, both in schools and in everything they read, that there was really no difference between pigs and wolves. The three little pigs were told that the wolf culture was just as good as the pig culture. Even though the wolf culture had never invented the car, or the steam engine, or the train, or the airplane, or the printing press, or discovered cures to many diseases that formerly killed pigs for thousands of years; or even though the wolf culture had no art, music or literature that people everywhere appreciated, they were told that the wolf culture was just as good, if not better than the pig culture.

In fact, the three little pigs were now taught that the wolf should not be called the "big bad" wolf anymore. They were taught that calling the wolf the "big bad" wolf was intolerant and insensitive to the wolf's feelings. They were told that the "big bad" wolf was a stereotype developed back in the day when pigs were intolerant and insensitive. The pigs were now taught in school that they should be sensitive to other creatures so all creatures could live in harmony. And so, the story of the "big bad" wolf no longer scared the three little pigs. In fact, in many places the story was no longer even told, for fear of offending the wolves.

And then one day the three little pigs looked around and noticed that they had a number of empty and unoccupied bedrooms in their big, old, beautiful house. It seems that the three little pigs had been taught how to give pleasure to one another without having to worry about a lot of little baby pigs showing up as a result. And so, there were lots of empty bedrooms in the big old beautiful house.

And then one day, Mr. and Mrs. Wolf actually came to the door. But they didn't say "Open up, open up and let us in, or we'll huff and we'll puff and we'll blow your house in!" No, they said, "If you let us into your house, we promise that we'll cook for you and clean for you and do all the chores around the house that you don't want to do, and since you have all those extra rooms, we'll sleep there and we won't be any inconvenience at all." And because the old story of the Big Bad Wolf had been forgotten, or dismissed as intolerant, the three little pigs thought this was a wonderful idea. They gladly opened the door to Mr. and Mrs. Wolf and they let Mr. and Mrs. Wolf into their house to live with them.

And after a while, the three little pigs noticed that Mr. and Mrs. Wolf had lots of little wolves running around their house. And Mr. and Mrs. Wolf said,

"You still have lots of empty bedrooms in your house, so now that we have little wolves, can we use some more of your empty bedrooms?" And the little pigs agreed and soon the big old house was all filled up with the three little pigs, Mr. and Mrs. Wolf and lots of little wolves.

And then one day, a strange thing happened. George Pig, Jr. came by the house and stood on the sidewalk. George Pig, Jr. was the caretaker of the largest house in the whole neighborhood. In fact, to the three little pigs, they thought his house was a mansion. George Pig, Jr.'s house was on the other side of the pond, but it was plain for all to see that no other house could compare to it.

But on this day, George Pig, Jr. was visibly agitated. He told the three little pigs that some Big Bad Wolves had driven a truck filled with dynamite into his house and lots of his fellow pigs were killed.

He said he knew which Big Bad Wolves had done it and he was going to make sure it didn't happen again. So he was going over to the other side of the tracks, where the Big Bad Wolves lived, and he was going to kill any wolf that was involved with that truck, including any wolf that owned the garage where the truck was parked before it drove over to his house and exploded.

George Pig, Jr. also said he knew about other wolves that driving cars filled with dynamite into other pig houses in other neighborhoods. He said these Big Bad Wolves were killing not only pigs, but other wolves, too. G.P., Jr. said he was going to kill them, too, so this whole business of driving cars and trucks into piggy houses and exploding them would stop. He added, "Sometimes pigs in smaller houses aren't strong enough to fight the Big Bad Wolves all by themselves. But the little pigs in his house *were* strong enough, so he would help the other pigs. In this way the Big Bad Wolves would not huff and puff anymore."

So G.P., Jr. said to the three little pigs, "I came by, because you live in a nice, big, old house and because you have been our friends for a long time, to see if you would help?"

For a minute, the three little pigs felt a rush of energy, for they had vague memories that at one time their parents were really good friends with the little pigs who lived in the big house across the pond, long before George Pig Jr. was the Caretaker.

But then they hesitated. They felt the presence of many wolf eyes looking at them from behind. The wolves had listened to the whole conversation. The wolves' staring, unblinking eyes and their presence in their home gave the three little pigs an uneasy feeling that they couldn't really describe.

Then they heard the breathing of the wolves behind them and the three little pigs huddled amongst themselves.

After some quiet discussion, the three little pigs said, "No thanks, George Pig, Jr. You are overreacting. You are a wild cowboy. Get help from somewhere else, we weren't the ones attacked."

G.P., Jr. listened, and though a bit bothered, continued on. He thought the three little pigs were underestimating the danger, but in his zeal to protect his own pigs, he was determined not to ignore the danger.

A number of years went by. G.P., Jr. got into a pretty good fight on the other side of the tracks. Then, George Pig, Jr. retired as the caretaker of the big house across the pond. A new caretaker was put in place. This new caretaker sought to placate the wolves.

Meanwhile, the baby wolves inside the big, old, nice house of the three little pigs became teenage wolves. And one day they looked around and saw all the nice things the three little pigs had, and how *they* had *no* nice things. And the teenage wolves said amongst themselves, "Many of us were born in this house, yet the three little pigs have all the nice things and we have none. That's not fair!"

So the teenage wolves went on a rampage. The young wolves wrecked a lot of things. But after a while the older wolves that first moved into the house got them to quiet down. You see, wolves are smart. They looked around and saw there were no teenage little pigs, and the three little pigs were getting old. So they kept still, knowing they could bide their time.

Meanwhile the wolves were *always* looking across the pond to the big old mansion on the other side. On past nights, they had seen the well-lit house alive with people. They could hear music, laughter and dancing.... The wolves thought of their own situation and seethed with rage.

But lately, things began to change. They could hear shouting and fighting inside the mansion across the pond. The new Caretaker got into a lot of arguments with the other pigs in the mansion. Rumors spread that the new

Caretaker had a wolf for a father and was therefore half wolf and half pig. There was shouting that all wolves should just be left alone. The new Caretaker went to where the wolves lived and apologized for his fellow pigs, and praised the wolves for their culture. And the wolves listened and smiled with approval.

Back at the home of the three little pigs, after the young wolves went on a rampage, the three little pigs all got together and decided that the wolves must be upset about their situation. So the three little pigs convened a meeting with the wolves.

The wolves demanded more of the things around the house they were used to. The wolves claimed the three little pigs were intolerant and insensitive to the plight of the wolves. The wolves complained that, in the past, the grandparents of the three little pigs had oppressed the wolves; so they wanted special consideration to make up for the past injustices. Many academic pigs agreed. So, over time, art, language, and even the laws governing how the pig house would be run, began to change.

And then one day, the three little pigs just disappeared. No one knows if they left to go across the pond, if they died, or if they were hiding in the basement.

But it wasn't long after that when the wolves decided that the art, music, literature and churches that were in the big old house when the wolves first moved in reminded them of pigs and not wolves. So, slowly over the years and the wolves changed everything around and soon, nobody spoke the language of the three little pigs anymore.

And it wasn't long after that when the Big Bad Wolves, much larger in number now, stronger and with a more aggressive attitude from that of their parent wolves, traveled across the pond and demanded of the new Caretaker, "Let us in, let us in, or we'll huff and we'll puff and we'll blow your house in!" And what did the new Caretaker of the mansion say? Was it, "Not by the hair of our chinny, chin, chin"? Or, like the three little pigs … did he just let them in?

All could see the new Caretaker was different. He *identified* with the wolves. He apologized for the pigs and said wolves would be treated differently from now on. He allowed any wolves that wanted to come into the mansion to, well, come in. And slowly, over time the music stopped (except for wailing sounds five times a day), the laughter died, and the lights went out. The big mansion on the other side of the pond went dark and was never heard from again.

* * * * * *

Europe has been softened up and lulled into a false sense of security by decades of tolerance and multiculturalism. Europe has lost its instinct for cultural self-defense in part because it sees no need for military self-defense. Non-judgmentalism and moral relativism run amuck, paralyzing its institutions from condemning conduct that oppresses women and restricts free speech.

Centuries ago in Southern Europe white women were prized features across the auction blocks of the Caliphate. It was then when the European soothsayer, Nostradamus, predicted "The camel will drink blood from the Rhine River." Is his prediction closer to reality than we think?

Chapter Three
They Are Coming For You Next
(A Religion of Peace?)

In Chapter 1 you read that the elected leader of the territory occupied by the Palestinians and the elected leader of the Iranian Islamic state openly declared their intention to destroy Israel, America and the West. There are some who suggest that if America eased off supporting Israel and sided more with nations that have issues with Israel, this would improve our relations with these nations and thus improve the prospects for peace. History proves otherwise. This theory of foreign policy will only lead to more aggression and more violence at the hands of the Islamic Supremacists. Appeasement simply allows the appeaser to be last in line to be devoured by the wolf, but the devouring remains the same.

My great-grandfather was a coal miner in southern Illinois. Miners learn the warning signs that tell of impending cave-ins or releases of poisonous gas. Canaries that live in the mineshaft will suffer from a mining disaster before the miners will. So when disaster is imminent the canaries will fly out of the mineshaft, or will be seen dead, warning the miners of impending doom.

Persecution of the Jews is the canary in the mine. The Nazi persecution of the Jews in the 1930s in Germany was at first considered a "German/Jewish problem." But the persecutions did not stop there. Next in line for death included the learning disabled, then gypsies, then Catholics, and then the enslavement and destruction of Germany's neighboring countries (by then deemed inferior as well). And so it is, and will be, with Islamofascists. Appeasement of this kind of hate only breeds more of it. The persecution of Jews is more often than not a harbinger of worse things to come for everyone, if not firmly opposed.

But hate for Jews, while a rallying point for Islamic Supremacists, is only one of many groups singled out for death or severe punishment by them. In Afghanistan in 2006, the legal system meted out the death sentence for a man whose only crime was his conversion from Islam to Christianity. Sharia law requires death for any apostasy—the renunciation of Islam. After world pressure exposed the Afghanistan's leaders' intents, the apostate was declared insane and mentally incompetent. This was the only reason his death sentence was commuted. He escaped and now resides in Italy.[37] But world pressure did not alter the enforcement of the law, nor did it change the law which was used to impose the death penalty.

In 2007 in Sudan, an elementary school teacher was sentenced to flogging for naming a teddy bear "Mohammad." This "crime" raises an interesting question: If Mohammad truly was the greatest of all prophets as Islam teaches, why must his name have to be so stridently guarded from insult? Would not his life and deeds alone be sufficient to withstand attack from schoolteachers and cartoonists?

Islamic intolerance of free speech and other religions is no recent phenomenon, however. What follows is not intended to be an exhaustive or in-depth discussion of the topic presented. It is only a cursory analysis of historical facts to accomplish two things:

1. Alert the reader to the danger we and our children face from Sharia compliant Islamists, and…
2. Encourage the reader to conduct his or her own research so as to be better equipped to interpret and respond to the unfolding of world events.

The Origins of Islam

Those schooled in Judeo-Christian scripture know about father Abraham. In Genesis, the first book of the Old Testament or Torah, Abraham's faith is tested by God when Abraham is asked to sacrifice his son Isaac to Him. Abraham builds an altar and affixes his son to it. At the last minute, as Abraham lifts his knife-wielding hand to slay his son, God intervenes and stays the hand of Abraham. God promises that Abraham's faith and obedience to God will be rewarded. "…because you have done this thing … I will bless you and … I will multiply your descendants as the stars of the heaven and … your descendants shall possess the gate of their enemies." The spared son, Isaac, is father to Jacob, whose name was changed by God to Israel, and the line establishing the sons and daughters of Judaism began. For Christians, the unbroken line continues through David, (slayer of Goliath) culminating in the birth, death and resurrection of Jesus Christ.

About a thousand years after Genesis was written—and a little more than five hundred years after the life of Jesus—Mohammad was born, slightly east of all of the foregoing events but within the same general biblical geographical area. Interestingly, every year around the same time that Jews celebrate Passover and Christians celebrate Easter, Muslims celebrate Eid ul-Ahda or the "Festival of Sacrifice."

This festival was written in the *Hadith,* a thousand years after Genesis was written. The Hadith is a collection of sayings and stories of Mohammed, considered equally as authentic as the Quran, the Muslim equivalent to the Bible. Eid ul-Adha also commemorates the story of Abraham who offered his son as a sacrifice on God's command. God stopped him and provided a sheep instead. However, *the Hadith declares that the son was ISHMAEL,* Isaac's younger half brother, who was birthed by Hagar, Sarah's maidservant, not by Abraham's wife Sarah, the mother of Isaac. The *Hadith* declares that Ishmael, the illegitimate son of Abraham, found favor with God and is the ancestor of all Arabs. He becomes the source for the Islamic claim that *it* is the one true religion and that therefore, Muslims are the chosen people.

Equally interesting is what the Bible says when Hagar found she was pregnant. Genesis 16: 11-12 states that an angel visited her. "And the angel of the Lord said unto her, Behold, thou are with child and shalt bear a son, and shalt call his name 'Ishmael' because the Lord hath heard their affliction. And he will be a wild man; his hand will be against every man, and every man's hand against him…"

Muslim Conquest Preceding the Crusades

At the time of Mohammad's birth, Christianity geographically encompassed, outside of Europe, the entire ancient Roman province of Asia, extending across the Caucasus Mountains to the Caspian Sea, to Syria, including the Holy Land, and a wide belt of North Africa from Egypt west to the Atlantic Ocean. Christians in the world numbered over thirty million by 311 CE. Most of them lived, not in Europe, but in Asia Minor and Africa. This geographical area was the home to such Christian fathers as Paul of Tarsus, Augustine of Hippo, Polycarp of Smyrna, Turtullian of Carthage, Clement of Alexandria, John Chrysostom of Antioch, and Cyprian of Carthage. The Seven Churches mentioned in Revelation (the last chapter of the New Testament) were all in Asia Minor. Smyrna was the last of these and she kept her Christian light burning until 1922 when the Turks destroyed it and annihilated its Christian population.[38]

Waves of conquest arising from the Muslim religion took place in the heart of these Christian lands. In the Muslim invasion of Syria in 634, thousands of Christians were massacred. In Mesopotamia (modern day Iraq), between 635 and 642 CE, monasteries were ransacked and the monks and villagers slain. Around this same time in Egypt, all Christians were put to the sword—before the Coptics repopulated the area. In Armenia, the entire population of Euchaita was wiped out. Muslim invaders sacked and pillaged Cypress and then established their rule by a great massacre. In North Africa, Tripoli was pillaged in 643 by Amr who forced the Jews and Christians to hand over their women and children as slaves to the Arab army. Carthage was razed to the ground and most of its inhabitants killed.[39] For the millions of Christians and Jews living in the Middle East in the 7th Century, with the advent of Islam, a long night descended on that region of the world. By the time of the First Crusade at the beginning of the second century CE, Muslims had succeeded in massacring and occupying by force of arms the entire geographical area of the early Christian Church. In Western Europe, the Muslims crossed the Pyrenees Mountains out of Spain and into France, promising to stable their horses in Rome! They were defeated, however, by Charles Martell at Tours, 100 years after Mohammad's death.

It is therefore necessary to suggest that history may have been re-written by Western apologists and Western academic elites. Most of us were taught that the Crusades were an example of Western imperialism. And while much of the Crusades involved wrongful slaughter of innocents, another reading of history reveals that the first Crusade was not a war of conquest but that of Christendom *striking back* at *Muslim* aggression.

Far from being wars of imperialist advancement, the Crusades were the *belated military responses* of Christian Europe to three centuries of Muslim aggression against Christian lands, the systemic mistreatment of the indigenous Christian population of those lands, and the harassment of Christian pilgrims. The post-modern myth, promoted by Islamic propagandists and supported by self-hating Westerners, notably in academia, claims that peaceful Muslims native to the Holy Land were forced to take up arms in defense of European-Christian aggression. This myth takes 1092 AD [CE] as its starting point, but ignores the preceding *centuries,* when Muslims swept through the Byzantine Empire, conquering about two-thirds of the Christian world at that time. For the Crusades, the driving impulse was not one of conquest and aggression, but of *recovery and defense* of the Holy Land in liberation of the Christians who, in many places, still constituted a majority of the population. The Crusades were a *reaction* to what the Muslims had done. Recognize the primary difference: The Crusader's wanton killings were *in disobedience* of their scripture. The Muslim killings were in *accordance* with their scripture.

Post Crusader Muslim aggression

As the centuries passed, Muslim aggression continued. The Crusader victories were but a temporary setback to Islamic expansion. Between 1200 and 1900, massacres in India at the hands of Islamists were greater in sheer numbers than all of the deaths of the Holocaust.[40] The reign and expansion of the Ottoman Empire reached its peak in the 1500s when it controlled Egypt, Syria, present-day Iran and as far west as the gates of Vienna in central Europe.[41] The Ottoman rule continued until the dissolution of the Ottoman Empire at the end of World War I.

It is amazing that in this age of rampant victimology, the persecution of Christians by Muslims has become a taboo subject in Western higher education. The silence and the half-truths perpetrated by the Western academies of higher learning and the media elite continue to blind the average person concerning the murderous history of Muslim expansionism.

Islamic law and its treatment of non-Muslims today

Scholars agree that according to Sharia law there is *no* concept of equality, human rights or even human dignity for non-Muslims.[42] Citizens are divided into three categories: (1) Muslims; (2) People of the Book (Jews and Christians); and (3) All others (all people in categories 2 and 3 are considered infidels). It is permitted under the Quran and Sharia law to kill infidels under certain circumstances. For People of the Book, according to Muslim jurists, the following ordinances must be enforced on Christians and Jews who reside among Muslims:

- They are not allowed to build new churches, temples or synagogues. Construction of <u>any</u> church, temple or synagogue on the Arabian Peninsula is prohibited. You will find no Christian churches in Saudi Arabia, least of all Jewish temples.
- In Saudi Arabia, it is illegal to wear any outward sign of Christianity.
- Muslims are permitted to demolish all non-Muslim houses of worship in any land they conquer.
- Jews and Christians are not allowed to pray or read their sacred books out loud, either at home or in churches, lest Muslims hear their prayers and be offended.
- Jews and Christians are not allowed to print their religious books or sell them in public places or markets in Islamic countries.
- Christians are not allowed to install a cross on their houses or churches because it is a symbol of infidelity.
- Christians and Jews are not permitted to broadcast or display their ceremonial religious rituals on radio or television or to

use the print or broadcast media to publish any picture of their religious ceremonies.

- Christians and Jews are not allowed to congregate in the streets during their religious festivals.
- Christians and Jews are not allowed to join the army. (I bet the families at Fort Hood sure wish the reverse was true.)

One only needs to observe present day Saudi Arabia to know the truth of the foregoing list. Yet, a double standard is apparent in today's world. In the tolerant West, Muslims are perfectly willing to use our tolerance and our laws respecting freedom of speech, freedom of assembly and freedom of the press to force our acceptance of their culture. But should they assume political control the reverse will not be the case. Note for example the Muslim demands to abolish freedom of the press and speech when it comes to the publication or utterances of things deemed offensive to Muslims. Tolerance is cultural suicide when it is a one-way street (see Chapter 5).

The West's response to the satirical cartoons which depicted Mohammad with a bomb for a turban was completely wrong. Most newspapers in western cities around the world and in the United States refused to publish the cartoons for fear of further reprisals and for fear of further offense to the Muslim community. This willingness to abdicate our freedoms, especially freedom of the press, will only lead to further repression of those freedoms so as not to "offend" our neighbors. Islamofascists will use our political correctness to their advantage. It is conceivable that, given present trends, if a Christian wanted to put a cross on his front lawn during the Christmas season, or if a Jew wanted to display a menorah, it would be considered a hate crime because it would show lack of sensitivity to the Muslim neighbor who happened to live next door (see Chapter 5).

Islamic law and its treatment of women today

A woman has been found guilty of adultery. She is buried from the waist up and her arms are tied to her sides in preparation for stoning. Tears cascade down her cheeks as the men shoveling the sand bury her just above her hips. With her arms at her sides this prevents her from any ability to use her arms to protect her head from the stones which will be shortly hurled at her. A legal ruling states that the stones should not be so large as to cause early death, but not so small as to not inflict pain. Sixty minutes later she is dead. Her adulterous male companion walks home.

Is this a scene in Persia played out 1,000 years ago? No. The country is Iran, and the year is 2007. The same scene is played out in any number of Islamic Sharia compliant countries today. How can this be?

Islam is dominated by a sexual morality derived from tribal Arab values dating from seventh century Saudi Arabia. It was a culture in which the women were property of their fathers, brothers, uncles, grandfathers or guardians. Today, it is still an offense if a woman glances in the direction of a man, brushes past his arm, or *shakes his hand*. A man's reputation and honor depend entirely on the respectable, obedient behavior of the female members of his family. Why didn't Mrs. Obama travel with her husband when he traveled to the Islamic countries of the Middle East, but instead, chose to remain behind in Europe to go "shopping?" I suggest they knew of and respected Islam's intolerance of women.

On February 28, 2008, *The Times* of London reported that in Saudi Arabia a university professor—a prominent and well-respected teacher of psychology at Umm al-Qra University in Mecca—was sentenced to 180 lashes and eight months in jail for having coffee with an unrelated female. Contacts between unmarried men and women are strictly forbidden. Religious police, known as *Mutaween*, under the command of the Saudi Commission for Promotion of Virtue and Prevention of Vice, routinely patrol public places to enforce the ban on communication between men and women outside the family.

Not long before, a 37-year-old American businesswoman and mother of three was thrown in jail for sitting with a male colleague at a Starbuck's coffee shop. In the same year—also in Saudi Arabia—a teenager was a victim of a gang rape. The teenage girl was sentenced to 200 lashes and *six years* in jail as a result. What was her crime? She was sitting in the car of an unrelated man.

How can this be? The problem began at the beginning. Mohammad was a polygamist and wrote that men have authority over women because God made one superior to the other. Most of the world thought that at the time. In Europe, however, the Enlightenment, the Age of Reason and the Renaissance came along. John Stuart Mill wrote that if freedom is good for men, it is good for women. The western world now considers this as the equivalent of an immutable truth. Yet, when Theo Van Gogh was murdered in 2003 for directing a movie critical of Islam in its treatment of women, there was no moral outrage from the Muslim community. More importantly, there was very little outcry from feminists in the West. When the Miss World Beauty Pageant was held in Nigeria in 2002, Islamofascists protested the holding of the pageant. When a Christian journalist wrote a response deemed offensive to the Prophet, the office of the newspaper was burned down, 200 people were killed and 500 people were injured.

Beyond the fact that the Enlightenment and the Age of Reason skipped over Islam, the Quran itself gives men the right to beat their wives. The Quran, Sura 4:34 states: "If you experience rebellion from the women, you shall first talk to them, then (you may use negative incentives like) deserting them in bed, then you may (as a last alternative) beat them."

On polygamy, the Quran says: "Marry women of your choice, two, or three, or four; but if you fear that you shall not be able to deal justly (with them), then only one." —Sura 4:30

Many Muslims will dismiss this verse, say it is taken out of context and is no longer applicable—that it was written at a time and place when polygamy was common. Such protestations are contradicted by the facts. See, for example, the article by David Rusin, "Take My Wives, Please: Polygamy Heads West." [43] In his article, Rusin reports that currently 30,000 Muslim families in France, 15,000 in Italy and several thousand in Great Britain include more than one wife. In fact, the British government has ruled that husbands can claim government benefits for multiple wives as long as the marriages are legal in the countries where they were conducted.

The push to normalize polygamy is yet another front in the Islamists campaign of stealth jihad, inch by inch. Tolerance is cultural suicide when it's a one-way street.

Muslim Persecution of Christians Today

In Iran today, Christian spiritual leaders are executed. In Lebanon, since 1975, *hundreds of thousands* of Christians have been massacred, displaced or exiled—due to its so-called "civil war."[44] Lebanon was a Christian-majority country only fifty years ago. Such is no longer the case. Did the Christians leave or were they exterminated by Islamic Supremacists?

In the Sudan, since its Islamic takeover in 1989, *one million* Sudanese have been killed because of their Christian faith. At one time, there were one million Christians in residence in Syria, but today it is a stronghold of Sharia Islam. In Egypt—as a result of British colonization—there were, at one time, millions of Christians in residence there. Where are they today? Who will succeed Mubarak? Certainly not the Christian Coalition. The Muslim Brotherhood wasted little time in gaining official control. Christians in Egypt are now persecuted and murdered by the hundreds.[45] In Indonesia, the Barrabas Fund reported at the end of 2000, a half-million Christians had been internally displaced, five thousand killed and seven thousand forcibly converted to Islam.[46]

A close examination of Islamofascist terror reveals significant similarities to its counterparts of the twentieth century: Nazism and communism. While the methods may have been different—the Nazis had their concentration camps and the communists had their gulags—the ideology remains the same. Islamic Supremacism, Nazi-fascism and communism all have in common the lust for other people's lives and property and the desire to exercise complete control over their subjects' lives. All three have been justified by a self-reverential system of thought and belief that perverts meanings of words, stunts our sense of moral clarity and destroys souls.

William Muir was an esteemed historian of Asia who lived between 1819 and 1905. At the end of a long and distinguished career of studying the Middle East, he declared his conviction: "The sword of Mohammad and the Quran are the most fatal enemies of civilization, liberty and truth which the world has yet known. They have combined to create an unmitigated cultural disaster, parading as God's will."[47]

Consider the words of Winston Churchill a generation later:

"How dreadful are the curses which Mohammedanism lays on its votaries. Besides the fanatical frenzy, which is as dangerous in a man as hydrophobia in a dog, there is this fearful fatalistic apathy.... Individual Moslems may show splendid qualities, but the influence of the religion paralyzes the social development of those who follow it.... Far from being moribund, Mohammedanism is a militant and proselytizing faith. It has already spread throughout Central Africa, raising fearless warriors at every step; and were it not that Christianity is sheltered in the strong arms of science, the civilization of modern Europe might fall, as fell the civilization of ancient Rome."[48]

Note Churchill's reference to the saving grace of the "strong arms of science." This refers to the West's technological superiority in weaponry and armaments since the late eighteenth through the twentieth century. Should Iran obtain nuclear weapons capability or other weapons of mass destruction similar to what was believed to have been possessed by Saddam Hussein in Iraq, Churchill's concern that the civilization of modern Europe would go the way of ancient Rome could well come to pass.

When the Mufti of Jerusalem declared at the Dome of the Rock in Jerusalem in 2001 that negation of Jewish existence was an existential need of Islam, he was and is reflecting a majority, main street Middle East Muslim position, continuing a well established tradition of more than a thousand years.[49]

Wake up, America! Do not let illegal immigration or our own apathy allow the sword of the prophet to destroy us. If the "People of the Book," as the Quran calls Jews and Christians, unite in their understanding of the threat we face and if we in the West have the moral courage to act, Judeo-Christianity will survive. So why is the media not warning us or reporting to us more on this danger? That is the subject of Chapter 4....

Chapter 4

The Enemy Within: Islamic Supremacists In The United States And Their Unwitting Collaborators: The Media And The Academic Left

(The Enemy of My Enemy Is My Friend.)

Part 1

News Flash: The Mainstream Media Is Not Telling Us the Truth about Islamic Supremacists

The misreporting and unwillingness of the mainstream media to tell us the truth about the war against Islamofascism begins with the premise that the mainstream media is leftist and overwhelmingly Democrat. As a result, the press and broadcast media are dually incentivized to misreport or negatively report the truth about the war on Islamofascism.

The Premise: The mainstream media is very left, very Democrat, and very out of touch with mainstream America. The leftward bias of the mainstream media has been extensively discussed and will not be repeated here to any great degree. The pioneer who first pointed out the donkey in the newsroom was Bernard Goldberg in his 2002 book, *Bias*, which became a *New York Times* bestseller, Goldberg was the first media insider to reveal what most Americans had suspected for a long time. He writes: "…there isn't a well-orchestrated, vast left-wing conspiracy in America's newsrooms. The bitter truth … is … worse." [50]

Goldberg was an insider for 28 years, so there were few more qualified than he to write his expose. A CBS news correspondent from 1972 until the summer of 2000, Goldberg knows the business and, as he wrote in his book, he knows what the news media does *not* want the public to see.

Here are some statistics from a survey conducted in 1996 by the Roper Center, a widely respected polling organization: In 1992, 89 percent of Washington, D.C. journalists voted for Bill Clinton, yet only 43 percent of the rest of the voting public chose Bill Clinton. Even the most disinterested observer of politics knows that *no* candidate gets 89 percent of the vote unless, of course, you are Fidel Castro or Hugo Chavez. In that same election, 7 percent of D.C. journalists voted for George Bush, Sr. even though *40 percent* of the rest of the country voted for him.

So, if nine out of ten journalists in Washington voted for a president that failed to garner even one-half of the rest of the nation's vote, can the media that reports the news coming out of Washington possibly be fair and balanced? The statistics get worse. Polling shows for those voters that indentify with a political party, the United States is about evenly divided between Republicans and Democrats. However, what percentage of journalists identify themselves as Republicans? Four percent of those that bring you the news identified themselves as such! And when asked to characterize their political orientation, 61 percent said liberal and 9 percent said conservative or moderate to conservative![51]

But this poll taken in the 1990's revealed nothing new. In 1972, a poll taken of the newsrooms showed that *70* percent of the journalists voted for Democrat George McGovern for President. Yet, in that election, his opponent, Republican Richard Nixon, carried every state in the Union except Massachusetts. That statistic bears repeating: Nixon beat McGovern in the popular vote in 49 states, yet over *two-thirds* of all journalists voted for Senator McGovern.

In March of 2000, the Orlando *Sun-Sentinel* conducted a poll of 3,400 journalists. The results were as follows:

The media are, as compared to the public-at-large:

- Less likely to get married and have children.
- Less likely to own homes.
- Less likely to go to a church or synagogue.

How many of the journalists polled belonged to the American Legion or service organizations like the Rotary Club? Zero.[52]

In 2007, a Harvard study conducted by the Shorenstein Center of the John F. Kennedy School of Government—not exactly a bastion of right-wing conservatism—came to the same conclusion.[53] This bias of the mainstream media was self-proven: the results of the study were largely unreported by the very media outlets exposed by the report.

The study examined 1,742 presidential campaign stories from January through May 2007. The survey included 48 different print, online, network TV, cable and radio news outlets. The conclusions spelled bad "news" for Republicans in two ways:

1. Democrats received more overall coverage than Republicans.
2. The tone of the coverage was more positive for Democrats. The difference was particularly severe in newspapers and on TV. Two-thirds of stories written about Democrats appearing on the front page of newspapers had a "clear, positive message"(about Democrats). Barack Obama's coverage was 70 percent positive! By contrast—for Republican candidates—26 percent of the coverage was positive. With regard to TV network news, the study showed they were equally biased. If you are surprised by this your left-wing bias is showing, or, you have recently returned from living in Canada. (Canadian news is so slanted, the *O'Reilly Factor* is banned!) On U.S. network TV, the greatest percentage of positive was for the Democrats at 40 percent. For Republicans, the opposite was true. Forty percent of the coverage was negative, with lesser percentages for neutral coverage or positive coverage.

There's more. Who said this? "I hope his wife feeds him lots of eggs and butter and he dies early, like many black men do, of heart disease." Was it a right-wing extremist? No, that terribly racist statement was uttered by a supposedly well-respected *USA Today* columnist, Julianne Malveaux. She got away with it because she was referring to a conservative. And who might that conservative have been? It was none other than U.S. Supreme Court Justice Clarence Thomas.[54]

Want still more? The *Los Angeles Times* printed an op-ed piece by Karen Grigsby Bates who was writing about then Senate majority leader of the U.S. Senate, Trent Lott: "…whenever I hear Trent Lott speak, I immediately think of nooses decorating trees. Big trees, with black bodies swinging from the business end of the nooses."[55]

However, when syndicated columnist George Will wrote in one of his columns, "I think it is reasonable to believe that (Bill Clinton) was a rapist," the *Los Angeles Times*—the same newspaper that allowed Karen Grigsby Bates to write, in essence, that Lott was a racist murderer—censored out of Will's article his comment about Bill Clinton.[56]

In July 2011, *Left Turn*, authored by UCLA Political Science Professor Tim Groseclose, chronicles in detail the liberal bias of all mainstream media outlets and how that bias shifts the average American's political views to the left![57]

Because our "War on Terror" was initially a Bush administration conflict, many in the media were loathe to report *anything* that might have reflected positively on its foreign policy decisions. The mainstream media only begrudgingly gave the Bush administration credit for things gone right, [58]but gave significant coverage to any event that showed things gone wrong.

The coverage of the so-called prison abuse scandal is a perfect example. The media reporting of Senator Durbin's remarks—the Senior Senator from Illinois—comparing the Bush Administration to the Nazi reign in Germany was actually portrayed as a serious comment.

How Muslim prisoners were being treated at Guantanamo was

never compared and contrasted to the *beheading* of reporter Daniel Pearl. American missteps, minor by comparison to human rights violations of other governments, are always examined in a vacuum of other human events. Islam gets a pass while we in the West are held to an arbitrary standard that is impossible to live up to. The United Nations sounds a call to close Guantanamo, where prisoners are given the Quran, but the Bible is not allowed so as not to offend the Muslims. The U.N. denounces America for its perceived human rights abuses while it barely acknowledges ethnic cleansing against Christians in the Sudan and gross abuses of human rights in Iran and other Muslim countries around the world.

This book is not an apologetic for the Bush Administration's foreign policy. However, the media bias begins in our colleges and universities, and goes far beyond simple disdain for all things Republican. Rather, the bias extends to a loathing of all things Western—as in Western civilization. This hatred has been the prevailing intellectual dogma spewed by colleges and universities throughout the country for over a generation. This anti-mainstream American dogma has been inculcated into the minds—and in some cases, the heart—of students for 40 years. Somehow, the cold judgment of history evidenced by the decline and fall of communism and other freedom-hating regimes has not mattered. Sean Hannity calls them the "blame America first" crowd. A sense of American exceptionalism has been lost. Unabashed American patriotism is ridiculed. What America stands for--its national identity and its role in world history—is no longer taught in a positive fashion.

Emerging from this intellectual incubator, many journalists today have no feel for the soul of America. They have no understanding of—as Alexis de Toqueville wrote almost 200 years ago in his *Democracy in America*—the fundamental goodness of America's people.[59] As a result, there is zero chance that the mainstream press can be "fair and balanced."

The American people instinctively sense this, which accounts for the overwhelming popularity of Fox News, which in turn only infuriates the mainstream media all the more.

It therefore becomes a rhetorical question as to whether bias in the media colors its presentation of the news, including the war on Islamic Supremacism. For example, why doesn't the media ask hard questions of the Islamists like, "In the ten years of continued Muslim terrorist activity all over the world since 9/11, what exactly is in the Quran that justifies murder?" Or, "Why are there no Christian, Jewish or Hindu suicide (homicide) bombers?"[60] I suggest you won't see in-depth news shows covering such topics because Islam would be cast in a negative light. Because Judeo Christianity falls short in their eyes, there must be something else that is better.

The Unspoken alliance between Islamofascism and the American Left

Is there then, what others have characterized as an "unholy alliance"[61] between the American Left—the media and academia—and Islamic Supremacists? The answer is yes: there does exist an unspoken affinity between the two groups, the Islamic Supremacists and the American Left. But why?

First, the hatred of American culture by the Left is much more virulent than the average American realizes. This antipathy by the Left of all things American actually goes back generations and was imported from Europe. The importation of this radicalism and instruction of anti-Americanism continues today.

Those that educate our children in our colleges and universities today came of age in the 60s during the height of the Vietnam War. In that time, they were taught by academics who were in colleges and universities in the 30s, during the Great Depression. It was in this hardscrabble environment that the socialist, anti-capitalist movement was at its peak in Europe and America.

Herbert Aptheker wrote and taught in American academic institutions in the 40s, 50s, 60s, 70s and 80s. His book, *History and Reality*, first published in 1949, became a foundational book for leftist historians that emerged after the Vietnam War. Therein, Aptheker wrote: "The global capitalist system is so putrid … that it no longer dares permit the people to live at all…. The American ruling class have the morals of goats, the learning of gorillas, and the ethics of… racist, war-inciting, enemies of humanity, rotten to the core, parasitic, merciless and doomed."[62]

Aptheker's venom might be dismissed if he had become irrelevant or had adjusted his belief system after the collapse of communism and the end of the Cold War. Oblivious, however, to the reality of real-world events as communist governments and state-run economies collapsed in country after country, and unmoved by America's technological advances and phenomenal rise in its standard of living in the 80s and 90s, Aptheker remained an unrepentant communist and an unabashed hater of all things American. He became the role model for the next generation of radicals and college professors that came after him.

In a sequence of events that would appall the average American— but perfectly acceptable in academic circles—Aptheker, at the end of his career in the 1990s, was given an appointment as a visiting professor at Bryn Mawr University and an appointment to one of the University of California's most prestigious law schools. Before his death in 2003, he was formally honored as a scholar by the History Department of Columbia University.[63] Aptheker was in his prime in the late 60s and his student disciples now rule the academy.

This writer went to college in the 1970s, specifically 1971 through 1975. As a political science major in a small, elite northeastern college, I took "Marxism," but "Capitalism" was never offered as a course of study. I obtained an "A" in Marxism because I learned how to regurgitate pro-Marxist, anti-capitalist dogma. I never believed any of it, but there were plenty of students that did. And now those students are in their fifties and sixties and find themselves as department chairmen and chairwomen of colleges and universities across America. If not in the academy, they occupy positions of influence on editorial boards of newspapers and TV stations around the country.

So today, we are witnessing the 60's generation of the Vietnam War protesters coming of middle age. They now occupy positions of authority, power and influence everywhere. Their mindset can be summed up as follows: Because America is an unjust society, all of its wars are unjust—period. Therefore, America's reasons for entering Afghanistan or Iraq are tainted *before* the fact. The fact that some say no weapons of mass destruction were found in Iraq only adds to their view of the war as immoral.

Recall the mainstream media's comments before the invasion of Afghanistan. A quagmire was predicted, like the Russian invasion before, and the excursion was doomed to failure. Before and during the surge in Iraq, the war was declared "lost."

Where are the leftists getting their higher education? The leading leftist institutions of higher learning in the United States, which one might even characterize as anti-American, are the Ivy League schools with the possible exception of Dartmouth, the University of California at Berkeley, the University of California at Los Angeles, the University of California at Davis, The City University of New York, and NYU.

Does this list of "prestigious" universities surprise you?

It should not.

Their lack of connectivity with the average American is the dirty little secret that allows alumni dollars to keep flowing back to those campuses. These are many of the feeder schools for American journalists and Washington elites.

Because the Left is out of touch with the average American they have largely failed at the election game. Before the 2008 election, a

Republican occupied the White House for 28 of the previous 40 years. The Left has also failed to capture the attention of working class American families. This, in and of itself, shows the Left's lack of understanding of democratic capitalism. In America, there is no permanent working class. America's unprecedented upward mobility of its people breaks the old Marxist stereotype of the "working class." Faced with the opportunity that any child in American can rise above the economic circumstances into which he or she was born, the siren song of wealth redistribution is resisted by most. As a result, the Left has turned to and has unfortunately succeeded in capturing the heart and soul of America's colleges and universities.

Who remembers Students For a Democratic Society? I do, because I was there. In 1969, in downtown New Haven, Connecticut—home to Yale University—I watched as the SDS literally started a riot. People were hurt, tear-gassed, and there was shooting. It was the ugliest thing I ever saw. The Doors wrote a song about it called "Peace Frog." One of the lines from that song was "Blood in the streets in the town of New Haven." The SDS were violent, angry, and they were anarchists.

One of its leaders, Todd Gitlin, is now a professor of sociology and journalism at Columbia University. He summed up the Left's academic triumph in the academy as follows: "My generation of the new Left—a generation that grew as the Vietnam War went on—relinquished any title to patriotism without much sense of loss…. The much-mocked 'political correctness' of the next academic generation was a consolation prize. We lost—we squandered—the politics, but we won in the textbooks."[64]

Well-renowned schools such as Harvard, Yale and the University of North Carolina offer courses such as "Whiteness Studies," "Cultural Studies," "Women's Studies," "African-American Studies" and "American Studies." In many cases, those courses and their names are euphemisms for a curriculum that is devoted to nothing less than a radical assault on American history and traditional American values.

Even law schools have been subverted by this political ideology. Consider the following passage from a legal text at an institution generally known as a very good law school—Georgetown. The legal text concerns the 14th Amendment, which makes the fundamental rights found in the U.S. Constitution applicable to individual states. The text states: "The political history of the United States that culminated and is reflected in the Constitution is in large measure a history of almost unthinkable brutality towards slaves, genocidal hatred of Native Americans, racist devaluation of non-whites, and sexist devaluation of women...."[65]

The above selective view of history fundamentally distorts America's influence on social mores and America's great heritage. More than two hundred years ago, America was the first country in history to reject a monarchy, throw off colonialism and declare all these "[t]ruths as self-evident. All men are created equal (under the law)."

This was revolutionary! About seventy-five years later, America literally tore itself apart in a civil war to end slavery. About fifty years later, America was in the forefront of another western-world revolution, when women were given the right to vote (1920). Over the next ninety years, Americans, by force of arms, force of will, and force of ideas, would liberate *millions* around the world from totalitarian tyrannies, never asking for anything in return other than an honorable burial for those who would not come home—and, in several cases, military presence—which provided protection to the inhabitants.

America's medical technology has healed and cured millions from diseases that have plagued mankind since the dawn of creation. America's economic order has provided more prosperity and more hope for more people than any society in the history of the world.

The average citizen needs to know, and our students must be taught, that the radicals in our media and universities are wrong. We must reclaim our heritage, reclaim our identity as a nation, and reclaim the vision for America. What is that vision? That America continues to be a city on a hill, a light to the world, and a beacon of hope for oppressed people everywhere. As Ronald Reagan said, "America, the last, best hope of man on Earth."

Returning now to the bias on university campuses, the bias is not only limited to a disdain for American capitalism. In addition to this virulent hatred for America is the concept of "moral relativism." "Moral relativism" is the belief system and worldview that all religions are equal, all cultures are equal, and all belief systems are equal, as long as such beliefs are sincerely held. This worldview contains no moral absolutes, otherwise some belief systems would then be considered unequal. Thus, from this environment of moral relativism springs political correctness. If all religions are equal, then no criticism of a religion can be tolerated. If you do criticize, you are intolerant. If you are intolerant, you are a bigot. Ergo: criticism of Islam causes you to be a racist and a bigot. But if you are a moral relativist who already hates Western society, it then becomes permissible to criticize America and Judeo-Christianity, but bigoted if you criticize Islam. Such is the state of our colleges and universities today.

Anti-American rhetoric from Islamic professors, imams and Muslim leaders is ignored. But sedition is not protected free speech. Yet, Islamic university professors are supported by their non-Muslim colleagues who belong to the "blame-America first" crowd in world affairs. Columbia University professor of anthropology and Latin America studies, Nicholas DeGenova, said, "U.S. flags are the emblem of the invading war machine in Iraq today. They are the emblem of the occupying power. The only true heroes are those who find ways that help defeat the U.S. military."[66] The American university has become the perfect place for the Islamic Supremacists to hide.

So, filter everything you see and hear through the prism of the bias from those that teach history and report current events, being aware of the environment of indoctrination from which they have been birthed.

Part 2

The Enemy Within: Islamic Supremacists in the U.S.

"We have met the enemy and he is us." —*Pogo*

No discussion of Islamic terrorism in the United States can begin without giving credit to Steven Emerson and his *Investigative Project on Terrorism*, first published over a decade ago. Serious students of radical Islam and its threat to Americans should begin with a study of his research.

Four planes, nineteen hijackers, well trained, well funded: more than three thousand murdered.

All of this mayhem accomplished, yet no alarms were sounded by the CIA, NSA, FBI, state police and others. How could this have been? It occurred because law enforcement at all levels *and* ordinary US citizens were largely unaware of the murderer living right next door. In the days and weeks after 9/11, Americans were aroused and vowed, "Never again!" Yet, ten years later, it appears that most Americans have rolled over and hit the snooze button on their alarm clocks. Fearsomely, our complacency has returned to pre-9/11 attitudes. We have become victims of our success in thwarting any large-scale terrorist attack directed toward American civilians. We must however, awaken again from our stupor and political correctness lest we awake on another sunny morning and witness the carnage of more 21st century barbarism.

The following account of a homicide bomber who killed an American teenager from Fort Lauderdale, Florida, in 2006—although occurring in Tel Aviv, Israel—could easily happen here unless we wake up to the danger from within.

PMF: State and spell your name.
TW: Tuly Wultz.
PMF: Mr. Wultz, where were you born?
TW: I was born in Jerusalem, Israel.

PMF: What year?

TW: March of 1954.

PMF: Where are your parents from?

TW: My mother is sixth generation Israeli and my father came from Hungry.

PMF: How many years is six generations?

TW: We'll assume it is about 200 years.

PMF: How did your mother and father meet?

TW: My father moved to Israel. At that time it was Palestine, right before the Second World War, and he met my mother in the Old City of Jerusalem and they both were teachers.

PMF: So, then, your mother was a resident of Palestine when Israel became a state.

TW: Yes, and so was my father, although he was captured by the Jordanian as a POW, defending the Old City of Jerusalem.

PMF: When was that?

TW: Just before 1948—when Jerusalem fell into Jordanian hands.

PMF: What war was that called?

TW: It was a pre-war for independence.

PMF: How long did you live in Israel?

TW: I was 26 when I left Israel and I came here. I met my wife in Israel and she brought me to America.

PMF: What year did you emigrate from Israel to the United States?

TW: At the end of 1979.

PMF: So your wife is an American?

TW: Yes. She is an American, second or third generation.

PMF: Where did you live during the 1973 War?

TW: I was a soldier already in the military and it was a tough war. I was already in officer's school and I was, of course, assigned back to my unit which we couldn't find, so I just joined whoever I could.

PMF: You were about 19 years old at that time. Is that right?

TW: Absolutely.

PMF: How long were you in the military service?

TW: Four years. Since I was an officer, I had to volunteer another year.

PMF: How did you meet your wife?

TW: Well, she went to Duke University Undergraduate and they had a very good department that did archeological digging in Israel and she decided to do that for credit and she was very interested in archeologically and she dug me up. (laugh)

PMF: So you got married here in the United States in 1981—is that correct?

TW: Correct.

PMF: And how long were you married before you had your first child?

TW: We were married about 5 years before we had the first child.

PMF: So your first child was born in 1986?

TW: The beginning of 1987.

PMF: And where was your first child born?

TW: Miami, Florida.

PMF: And was that a boy or a girl?

TW: It was a girl—it is a girl; a beautiful one.

PMF: Where does she live now?

TW: She's a student at the University of Miami.

PMF: Then you had another child after that. Is that right?

TW: Yes, we had another child, Daniel, and he was born in 1989.

PMF: And where was he born?

TW: At the same hospital in Miami.

PMF: Now, in 1989 you were living in Miami. What was your occupation?

TW: I was still doing insurance and financial planning.

PMF: Did your wife work outside of the home?

TW: Yes. She's a lawyer and she was working. She had her own law firm at that time.

PMF: Your wife is obviously an American citizen; your children are and were American citizens. Are you an American citizen?

TW: Yes, a naturalized citizen.

PMF: Where were you when you took your oath?

TW: It was in Miami Beach Convention Center.

PMF: How did you feel?

TW: I felt very proud. I felt kind of silly that I had not done that before because it really doesn't—it didn't—require me to give up my Israeli citizenship, so I should have done it before, but I didn't.

PMF: Was your wife there?

TW: Everybody was there even my kids, my in-laws.

PMF: Was there a big celebration?

TW: We had a huge party here.

PMF: When you say here, where is here?

TW: In my home, in Weston.

PMF: What family members were in attendance the day that you became an American Citizen?

TW: At the ceremony?

PMF: Yes.

TW: My in-laws, my children and my wife.

PMF: When you became an American, how did that make you feel?

TW: I felt very proud. I felt that I should have done it earlier. I feel that I can contribute more even if it is spiritually by that time because I did contribute a lot to the country. I think I was very successful in my business and by paying taxes I think it is one good way to help the economy and to help America.

PMF: What about America that makes you feel proud to be an American as someone who was not born here?

TW: Well, coming from a place that everybody tries to kill you everyday, there's a whole story about trying to be killed—that's a side story. Coming to America, everybody is free, you're really not worried about outside enemies. It is a very special feeling. And it is a feeling that I felt when they asked me, before I got my citizenship, if I would bear arms and protect this country. I had no hesitation to say of course. And I meant it with all my heart. I don't think that people who are born here and take American freedom for granted can really understand the freedom. Freedom doesn't come free. It is not a free commodity. Freedom you have to fight for it. And you have to protect whatever you have. And we have here in America everything that we need. But we have to protect it. And I felt that it would be an honor to come to a country that accepted me and so nicely and with open arms that I would definitely bear arms to protect this country.

PMF: Now, Mr. Wultz, in September of 2001 were you still working in America in insurance and financial planning?

TW: Yes. I've been working since 1981.

PMF: Before the events of September 11th, had you brought your children to visit Israel?

TW: Oh, yes. They came with me most of the times unless I went there just for a quick wedding or just a quick visit to my parents, but they loved it there. Especially Daniel. He was very happy going there because in Israel, unlike here in the United States, there are no distances. It is a small tiny country. So you walk everywhere. Most people where I lived, live in apartments and there are a lot of kids his age so they just disappear—somewhere. So he felt very free and kind of at home there, too. But I'm not sure he would leave there for a long time because he loved the life here.

PMF: When was the last trip that you made to Israel with Daniel?

TW: That was April of 2006.

PMF: And who were you with there? Was it just you and Daniel?

TW: No, it was Sheryl, Daniel and myself. Amanda was at that time at Tufts University in Boston and she was doing her finals, so she couldn't go with us. We really wanted to go to spend Passover with my family especially with my father because he wasn't doing well; being at that time 96 years old. We wanted to at least celebrate what we thought, was the last Passover with him.

PMF: In April of 2006, how old was Daniel?

TW: 16 and a half.

PMF: Where did he go to school?

TW: He went to David Pasnack Hebrew Day School in Plantation.

PMF: What grade was he in?

TW: Daniel was in the tenth grade.

PMF: Was he a good student?

TW: He was a very good student. Studies didn't come easy for Daniel. He was ADHD and he was fighting for every piece of information that he could remember and he was studying very hard. So he was a great student, but he had to work for it very hard.

PMF: What were his favorite subjects?

TW: Well, it's hard to say. He loved everything there at school.

PMF: Did he like to play sports?

TW: Oh, yes. He was a very good basketball player.

PMF: Did he have a lot of friends?

TW: He had tons of friends. Daniel was a very special boy. He was a very popular kid in school, but he didn't use his popularity to advance himself. Actually, he used his popularity to bring kids who were not popular into the group of the popular kids. He was very sensitive. He wanted to make sure that everybody is happy—everybody has a chance. He was a big fighter for justice. He wasn't a big boy—he was very strong but not a big boy and if he saw … in school, or out of school, kids are bullying somebody he was there right away to protect. He didn't look for fights. He never wanted to fight. He just protected the kids who were underdogs. The teachers were always amazed. They said you know, Daniel will one day get hurt protecting somebody else. And Daniel said he knew that. But he didn't care because he said if I don't protect them who will. If he would go in the street and he saw … I remember going with him to Publix and he saw an older man trying to carry a bag a groceries from the store—Danny went to him. He said, "Can I help you?" The man looked at him like he was from the moon. He said, "Where did you come from?" That was Daniel. He helped everybody and he became, of course, very spiritual towards the last two years of his life.

PMF: Now in April of 2006 why did you decide to take a side trip from Jerusalem to Tel Aviv?

TW: Sheryl, my wife, wanted to go shopping in Tel Aviv, after we met some friends of ours who live in Tel Aviv. So she went shopping. We went with her until Daniel was hungry.

PMF: Where did you stay when you went there?

TW: We stayed in a small hotel in Tel Aviv, by the ocean.

PMF: What was the name of the hotel?

TW: Apartment Hotel.

PMF: So you spent your first night in the hotel. Describe for me the events of that second day in Tel Aviv in April of 2006?

TW: In the morning when we got up, I took that picture of Daniel (points to picture). You can see the ocean right from the window. We decided to go … instead of going for a walk to the ocean just go right to the shopping and since I am not familiar with Tel Aviv, I left the rental car at the hotel and we stopped a cab. The cab driver took us almost to the place where he was supposed to take us, but he made an unreasonable mistake, we just don't understand why he brought us to that area, which is the old bus station of Tel Aviv. It's called the Nevshanan. It's an old neighborhood with a lot of foreign laborers who come to Israel to do labor jobs. But the cab driver, when he stopped the cab and he said, "You know what, I made a mistake … you can walk…. I cannot make a U-turn but you can walk to the place you want. It will take you less then ten minutes. By the way here is a restaurant, a schwarma place, probably the best in the country."

PMF: What is schwarma?

TW: It's usually lamb and turkey on a skewer that goes around, flavored in the middle eastern flavor. It tastes very good. Since then, I cannot eat that anymore. Daniel loved schwarma. And that's all that the driver had to say and he jumped out of the cab and went to the schwarma and asked them if they are going to be open for lunch. And, of course, they assured him that they will. He made sure that they are kosher for Passover because at that time it was Passover and he said to them I'll be back for lunch. And we walked around with Sheryl and then we walked around by ourselves. Daniel and I walked around this area of Tel Aviv and lunchtime came and Daniel said he was hungry. I remember the walk we took through the flea market of that area that led to the restaurant. It was really … not a desirable place to shop and not a desirable place to be but it was interesting nevertheless. Finally we got to the schwarma place, to the restaurant. It's called Rosh Haeer. It means "Mayor."

PMF: Was this a well-known restaurant?

TW: For a lot of people, yes. For us it was not because it is really a hole-in-the wall. There's no place to sit in that restaurant. It's not really a restaurant. It's like a kiosk that sells the schwarma and then you sit on the sidewalk.

PMF: So the tables are actually outdoors on the sidewalk?

TW: Correct.

PMF: Is it surrounded by any type of fence so that people who are not patronizing the restaurant are kept away?

TW: Yes. Absolutely. They built a very low fence, you could jump over it. It just marks the area of the tables—as you said so the people who are not patronizing the place won't sit there. So we sat … we had a table right at the entrance of…

PMF: Is there any kind of security at the entrance to the restaurant?

TW: Yes. We just sat down there and there was an older man who was a security guard. In Israel, unfortunately, most of the restaurants hire security to check people before they come in. It didn't make much sense to have the security guard over there by the gate but that's where he was and we were sitting right near him.

PMF: How many other people were sitting down?

TW: There were about—I would say close to 100 people.

PMF: So this was not a little sidewalk café?

TW: No.

PMF: What time of day were you there?

TW: It was 12. Around 12-12:10.

PMF: So when you walked up did the security guard—what do they do with an average customer?

TW: First of all, they look at you and then ask you if you are carrying anything. They want you to open your bag. Show them what is inside and if it is satisfying then they let you in.

PMF: So you went in?

TW: We went in. We bought the schwarma. We sat by the table that was free—actually we had to wait a few minutes for the table. When the table became free we sat there and Daniel who was a catsup king we called him, went back to the little kiosk to ask for extra catsup. When he was there, I saw this teenager, dark-haired looking guy, could fit any description of an Israeli Middle Eastern young guy of middle eastern descent. He was stopped by the guard like everybody else and the guard asked him what he wants.

PMF: How did you know that the guard asked him that? Could you hear?

TW: Yes—he was about three or four feet from me.

PMF: Did you observe him approaching the guard?

TW: Not really. I was busy eating my schwarma, but when he approached the guard, the thing that caught my eye was that he couldn't—he wouldn't answer the guard. He wouldn't talk to the guard. He pretended that he was mute and deaf and he showed with his hand to his mouth that that's what he wanted—showed that he was interested in eating. At that time Daniel came. And I felt concerned for the guy who couldn't speak. And I kept looking at him and the guard asked him to open his bag. When the guard asked him to open his bag he had an evil smile on his face when he— by the way, I didn't mention this before, he had a back pack which he laid on the floor while he was talking to the guard. Apparently, it was very heavy. It had I think about 40 pounds of explosives. So when the guard asked him to open the bag, he had a real evil smile on his face. And he pretended to go down to the bag. At that point

I knew that was a suicide bomber.... (Pause)

(Break for witness to compose himself.)

TW: When I recognized what he was going to do, I tried to shove Daniel and tried to get up from my seat to jump over Daniel, over the table but at that point, the terrorist detonated his bomb in his hand, I guess by remote and I flew backwards—because we were the closest to the bomb beside the security guard. Daniel flew right into my arms, and we fell on the floor. Daniel was screaming, "Pick me up, pick me up!" He had no idea what hit us. I realized what hit us and I tried to get up but I realized that I had no leg. My left leg was almost not there. But anyhow, with the rest of my power, on my knees, I took Daniel and put him on the floor and told him, "Daniel, you are hurt, please stay on the floor, help will come very soon. Give me your hand." He gave me his hand and I told him, "Daniel, I love you." And he told me, "I love you too, Dad." I looked at his back and it was like a strainer. Blood poured out, holes, tremendous holes and what he did, is actually he protected me with his beautiful body. He took most of the bomb shrapnel into his body and what ever was left, I took. Although a lot of the shrapnel came through his body to me, but for me it wasn't life threatening because it already hit him. Help came very fast. They took Daniel right away because I was shouting there is a little boy—I shouted in Hebrew little boy badly hurt, badly hurt. And they came and took him first, or among the first and then they came to the rest of the people, which at that time there were nine people who were killed on the spot, not including the terrorist, and about 64-68 other people were injured. So Daniel was taken right away to the hospital and when they came to pick me up, they knew who I was. They said, you're the father of that boy—yes, we're taking you to the same hospital. And they took me to Ichilov Hospital; it's in the middle of Tel Aviv. Daniel had already arrived. He went right into surgery. And at that time I lost my consciousness. I regained consciousness in the emergency room where I was and they cleaned me and prepared me for surgery myself. And I remember the doctor saying, "I think we can save your leg, I think we can save your leg and don't worry." I had shrapnel in my head, but he said, "I don't think it got to your brain. You can talk, you can move your arm. We don't think your brain was hurt, don't worry." I could hardly see anything because the blood was gushing over my eyes. Both my eardrums were blown out and later on we discovered that also there were some bones inside my head were shredded. That's why I can't hear well and I almost couldn't hear at all at that time. That's what really happened at that time. Daniel—the first surgery was 12 hours—three teams worked on him, and they wouldn't give up because he was conscious surprisingly when he went to the hospital and he told the anesthesiologist—he told her, "My name is Daniel Wultz. I'm from America and I want to live. I don't want to die." She was so impressed by that that she decided that they are going to fight for him. His first night he was given over 200 blood units, which is unheard of. It's so unheard of that a few days later when I was conscious enough I had a visitor who is an emergency room doctor from Mt. Sinai Hospital in New York—who said, "I just came back from the intensive care unit and I saw your son. Let me tell you something." He said, "There is no hospital in the world, and I can guarantee you in America, that would even treat your son in the shape that he came in." He said, "This is an amazing hospital." And Daniel was a fighter—unbelievable. And I mentioned before that he was practicing basketball all the time and his body was very strong and that's why he survived 27 days. The doctor's course of action when they learned about his body that was so strong, they took it in consideration to keep fighting just because they thought he could make it—and unfortunately he didn't.

PMF: After 27 days?

TW: Yes. I think it is important to describe the last day and last night.

You know, I didn't mention, but we immediately flew our daughter to Miami and with my wife's parents, they flew the next day to Tel Aviv. And my daughter never left Daniel's side—Daniel's bed; I mean just to eat and sleep. The last night his doctors called us to the conference room at the ICU and the doctor said that we lost the war. Daniel is not going to make it through the night. The infection just—he lost his kidney, he lost part of the liver, he lost part of his spleen, he lost a leg, he lost a hand, along with fingers; slowly, slowly, everyday they cut off another finger. But there was leaking blood all the time from his inside.

PMF: Internal bleeding.

TW: Yes. All the time through the holes that he had. Stopping that and stopping—and doing his dialysis because the other kidney was shut although it was not badly hurt, it wouldn't function so they had to give him dialysis every day. So somewhere he got—I mean the infection—all the shrapnel that came into his body—into everybody's body was purposely dirty and caused tremendous infection. Daniel had no immune system because of the hundreds of blood units that he received. There was no blood in his type any more so they gave him blood not his type to keep him alive. So the night the doctors called us—I remember we all came into the room, my in-laws, my wife, my brothers, my daughter and I and he said, "Daniel is not going to make it," and then Amanda said, my daughter, "But he's my only brother." And the doctors looked at her, and both crying, they couldn't say anything. They were devastated. Of course, Daniel, fought that night, and he didn't die that night. He died at 12:20 the next noontime. At that time we were all around his bed, singing his favorite songs. It was really a horrible experience, but a great way to say good-bye to him. And, in the course of this, while he was fighting for his last breath, my daughter said to him, "My first born will be named Daniel, I promise you that."

PMF: What was the last thing that he said to you? Was it at the café?

TW: Yes. When I told him I loved him and he said, "I love you, too, Dad."

PMF: Was the suicide bomber ever identified?

TW: Oh, yes. And not only identified, his mother went on Al Jazeera TV praising, not the Lord, praising Allah; that finally the dog died. And she can't wait to send her two daughters also to be suicide bombers. She was so proud of her son.

PMF: So, you've actually seen the television....?

TW: No, I couldn't see it. I mean I looked at it and then I turned away, I just couldn't see that. But I know it was there. I saw a lot of emails after that from some bad intentioned Muslims who praised the mother for her brave appearance on Al Jazeera and congratulated her.

PMF: Where is Daniel buried today?

TW: He is buried in Hollywood, Florida, at Beth David Memorial.

* * * * * * *

Could the foregoing account of such a despicable act of violence happen here? Fort Hood, Times Square and Detroit Airport give us our answer. We *must* identify our enemy. But where does the fomenting, planning and funding take place? One need only turn to the buildings that house those that worship a God called Allah....

Mosques and Islamic Centers

America has a long history of non-governmental interference with the practice of religions. Traditionally, religious and clerical institutions have not only been left alone by our government, but encouraged to exist—through taxation policies—because it has been generally understood, and rightly so, that such religious institutions, arising primarily out of the Judeo-Christian tradition, were and are forces for good. Hospitals, orphanages, shelters, soup kitchens and thousands of other such charitable endeavors have provided food, clothing, shelter and spiritual sustenance to millions. Private charitable giving in the United States, either through foundations, religious institutions or individuals, exceeds that of all other countries. The United States' citizenry has been the largest private charitable giver in the history of civilization. Unfortunately, with the rise of Islamic Supremacy, the concept that religious institutions are a force for good within the United States must be re-examined.

Islamic mosques or centers are led by imams, similar in concept to rabbis, priests, ministers and pastors. Many imams throughout the world have been trained in Saudi Arabia. The largest university for the training of imams is found in the Saudi Kingdom. It is the Mohammad ibn Saud Islamic University (SIU), located in Riyadh, Saudi Arabia. The school is the largest Wahabbi University in the world. Of importance to all Americans is the fact that at least two—and maybe as many as nine—of the 9/11 hijackers were graduates of this university. In January of 2004, the State Department revoked the diplomatic visas of sixteen people affiliated with the SIU's branch campus in Fairfax, Virginia because it was "promoting a brand of Islam that is intolerant of Christianity, Judaism and other religions."[67] Frank Gaffney, President of the Center for Security Policy and renowned expert on the threat to domestic security from Sharia compliant Islamists, states that 81 percent of United States mosques promote jihad.

Intolerance of Christianity and Judaism, and violence against infidels, is preached weekly in mosques across the United States. Radical mosques that teach hate on a weekly basis can be found in Pompano Beach in Broward County, Florida; Chicago, Illinois; Brooklyn, New York; Fairfax, Virginia; Portland, Oregon—and soon, in a town near you. The groundbreaking for a new mosque happens every week somewhere in the United States.

Joe Kaufman is a frequent columnist for FrontPageMag.com and founder of Americans Against Hate and CAIRWatch, and over the past five years, has been researching terrorism in the United States.

In a January 22, 2007 interview, Joe was asked: "Do you believe that there are mosques within the United States that are fronts for terrorist organizations?"

Joe responded: "The vast majority of the mosques in southeast United States are havens for radical Islam because of the circumstances under which they came about. The individuals that lead these mosques, the Board members that lead these mosques, the radical speakers that they have that pass through each of these mosques, and the organizations that created the mosques in the first place, all of these lend towards radical behavior that could possibly result in a terrorist attack."

In response to a question as to whether radical Islam within the United States is currently a threat to the peace and security of U.S. citizens, Mr. Kaufman stated:

Oh, yes, with the number of mosques that are going up year after year after 9/11, there is a definite threat inside the U.S. and it's only growing, it's not lessening, because the United States refuses to take action against any of the mosques, including the ones that have been involved with Al-Qaeda, that have been involved with the 1993 bombing of the World Trade Center or 9/11. So until the United States starts to crack down and maybe shut some of these places down, they're just going to be popping up over and over again.[68]

Unnamed sources within the FBI tell me that guns and ammunition can be found in almost every mosque in the United States. More concretely, in recent cases brought against Islamic terrorist cells within the United States, one commonality appears—the connection between the terrorist cell's members and a local mosque. The six men of the Al-Qaeda sleeper cell in Lackawanna, New York—who were arrested by the F.B.I. in 2001 for attending an Al-Qaeda terrorist training camp in Afghanistan—all belonged to the same Lackawanna mosque. One of the six who was arrested, Sahim Alwan, was the former imam of the Lackawanna Islamic mosque. The six men grew up in the Yemeni community of Lackawanna, Pennsylvania. They were recruited by Kamal Derwish, a Yemeni American who was teaching about Islam in the Lackawanna Islamic mosque.

In Florida's Dade and Broward counties, an imam and his two sons were arrested on May 14, 2011, charged with funneling money to the Pakistani Taliban in a long-running conspiracy to murder, maim and kidnap people in foreign terrorist organizations.

A Sunni mosque in suburban Beaverton, Oregon was the meeting ground for six members indicted by federal authorities in 2002 for conspiring to provide aid to the Taliban and Al-Qaeda terrorists. FBI documents allege the imam of the mosque, Sheik Mohamed Abdirahman Kariye, used $12,000 collected from the members of the mosque to fund the efforts of the "Portland Six" to join the Taliban. A second Oregon mosque, also in Beaverton, collected thousands of dollars from its worshipers by claiming that the money was needed to help the parents of two members of the mosque in Saudi Arabia. In reality it was to finance their trip to join the Taliban.[69]

The Al-Farooq mosque in Brooklyn has been in the public spotlight for more than ten years as a hotbed of Islamic radicalism, sedition and treason. The imam there, Sheik Omar Abdel-Rahman, was convicted in 1995 of conspiracy to bomb New York City landmarks. The Al-Farooq mosque collected money that was personally delivered to Osama bin Laden.[70] Abdel-Rahman was also a regular speaker at the Al-Salaam mosque in Jersey City, New Jersey, where many of the suspects in the 1993 World Trade Center bombing regularly worshipped.

In 2003, Amin Awad, a Muslim chaplain who counsels inmates in New York's Ryker's Island jail, was reassigned because of his links to terrorist fundraising. Just before his reassignment, Awad was named President of the board of trustees at the Al-Farooq mosque.

American mosques are regular stops on fundraising trips for terrorist leaders and their sympathizers. Osama bin Laden's chief deputy, Ayman Al-Zawahiri, made at least two money-raising trips to the United States in the 1990s, collecting money at various mosques along the way. Prominently featured were mosques in Santa Clara, Stockton, and Sacramento, California.

Mosques in the United States are no different than mosques across the world. Militant Islam operates in mosques everywhere as their central meeting place. In reviewing the movie, *Obsession: Radical Islam's War Against the West*, imams are quoted throughout the Middle East preaching their special brand of hate, violence and murder against Israel, the United States and all infidels. It is no accident that most US mosques have become appendages of this worldwide jihad against the West.

At the end of World War II, there were about fifty mosques located in the United States. Today there are more than 1,300—and the number grows monthly.

But building mosques costs money.

Where does that money come from?

Follow the Money

The money comes from all of *us*. The money is generated by the sale of oil, and oil is refined to create gasoline—gasoline that powers America. Because our politicians have consistently voted for more than thirty years against drilling for more oil in Alaska, off the coast of Florida, and for oil shale in the mountain states, the United States today imports 70 percent of its oil. President Obama's executive orders have only increased the areas banned from drilling. We are financing the very terrorists that seek to destroy us!

The Saudis built more than 60 percent of the mosques constructed in the 1980s and 1990s. According to one estimate, by 2002 the Saudis had spent more than $70 billion to fund 80 percent of the mosques built in the United States in the last 20 years.[71] One of those mosques, the Bilal Islamic Center in Los Angeles, California, was one of the addresses given by Mark Fidel Kools, also known as Asan Akbar, the 101st Airborne sergeant who killed a fellow serviceman and wounded 15 others with a grenade in Kuwait shortly after the Iraq war began in March, 2003.

And if Saudi money is not available, in the case of Sh'ia mosques, Iranian money is there to step into the vacuum. Americans, by and large, continue to be uninformed, completely unaware that the mosque a block from the corner convenience store could this very night be planning the next bomb attack.

Islamic "Charitable" Organizations

CAIR (Council on American Islamic Relations): According to court documents recently made public, CAIR raised money for terrorist charities prior to 9/11 and is listed as an unindicted co-conspirator in the Holy Land conspiracy trial. Many of its leaders have been charged with terrorist activity.

One national board member of CAIR was listed on the U. S. Attorneys' list of potential co-conspirators in the 1993 bombing of the World Trade Center. And yet, CAIR, of all organizations, actually conducted Islamic sensitivity training for the FBI.

The Muslim Student Association, an innocuous sounding name, also supports and funds Islamic Supremacists in the United States. These individuals understand America's brand of political correctness and the tolerance of "free speech" in academic circles. They use it to their advantage. Islamic Supremacists know that, in the name of tolerance, universities and colleges will turn a blind eye to any Islamist propagandizing, teaching or seditious activities. The Islamic Supremacist holy war in America (which some have called stealth Jihad), is America's Trojan horse. It is the elephant in the room that nobody wants to recognize. It is the emperor who has no clothes that no one wants to acknowledge. They have and continue to insert themselves into our textbooks, academia and other institutions. Any attempt to criticize their own brand of hate speech is met with the charge of racism and bigotry, effectively silencing any opposition.

Other Islamic charities also act as fronts for the collection and distribution of American dollars to teach radical Islam and foment sedition. The Islamic Association for Palestine (IAP) is a Hamas front. Yet, its leader, Abu Marzook, was welcomed at the Clinton White House and had top-level briefings there.[72] Prior to that, tax records show that Abu Marzook donated a cash payment of $210,000 to the Holy Land Foundation for Relief and Development. A raid on a Hamas center in 1992 in Jenine, Israel uncovered a cache of Holy Land Foundation documents identifying the organization as an arm of Al-Qaeda. Since the conviction of the Holy Land Foundation, the charities intent and plan for world domination by the Islamists has now been revealed. Below is the seven-step plan for world domination by Islamic Supremacists as offered into evidence by the Federal prosecutors in the Holy Land Foundation trial.

Seven-Step plan for world domination

Ayman al-Zawahiri's July 9, 2005 letter to Abu Musab Zarqawi is consistent with the thinking attributed to the radical Islamic leaders surrounding him, and the stages of action he lays out are consistent with their strategic game plan, which includes seven stages leading to the ultimate victory of Islam over the West in 2020. These stages are:

1. The "awakening," which refers to the attacks of 9/11, designed to make the Islamic movement a central player on the global scene;

2. The "opening the eyes," the period from 2003 to 2006 that will transform al-Qaeda into a "mass movement";

3. The "arising and standing up," the period from 2007 to 2010 that will focus on terrorist destabilization of existing Muslim regimes;

4. The toppling of the moderate regimes of Egypt, Jordan, Turkey and other Muslim states from 2010 to 2013;

5. The formation of a new world order between 2013 and 2016, based on an Islamic Caliphate as a world power and the weakening of the United States and Israel;

6. A total confrontation between Islam and the West in 2016-2020; and

7. A "Decisive Victory" for Islam in 2020.

Source: "The Zawahiri Letter and the Strategy of Al-Qaeda" b Shmuel Bar and Yair Minzilil, *Current Trends in Islamist Ideology, volume 3*, February 16, 2006, Hudson Institute.

Compare Item #4 above with the events of 2011 in Tunisia, Lybia, Egypt, Syria and Yemen. It appears that the Islamic Supremacists are right on track and following their plan exactly.

Prisons

Chuck Colson first gained fame (or infamy) when he was special counsel to the president of the United States, and was sentenced to prison for his obstruction of justice and other crimes arising out of the Watergate activities under the

Nixon administration. Following his prison experience, Chuck Colson founded a non-profit organization entitled, "Prison Fellowship," and has dedicated the past twenty years of his life to spreading the Gospel of Jesus Christ inside our prison system (wherever and whenever the prison authorities will allow, which in many states is restricted).

Colson's experiences in the prison system within the last ten years have enabled him to observe first-hand a very frightening development. Many Muslim chaplains are hard at work recruiting Hezbollah, Hamas and Al-Qaeda terrorists within our prisons and, upon the conclusion of their prison terms, inserting them into mainstream society. When it comes to Islam, all religions are not equal. It has been hundreds of years since Christianity espoused violence as a way to bring followers to its cause. For Judaism, it has been more than 2,000 years. Yet, reformation has not been introduced to Islam. Muslims have shown no reluctance when it comes to using death, mayhem and violence to promote their ideology.

Chuck Colson confirms that radical Muslims are hard at work in our country's prison system recruiting converts.

> Alienated, disenfranchised people are prime targets for radical Islamists who preach a religion of violence, of overcoming oppression by Jihad … (T)he radical fundamentalists—some of whom are invading our prisons—mean it literally. Those who take the Koran seriously are taught to hate the Christians and the Jew; lands taken from Islam must be recaptured. And to the Islamist, dying in a Jihad is the only way one can be assured of Allah's forgiveness and eternal salvation.[73]

He further states: "Al Qaeda training manuals specifically identify *America's prisoners* as candidates for conversion because they may be 'disenchanted by their country's policies.' As U.S. citizens, they will combine a desire for 'payback' with an ability to blend easily into American culture."[74]

For South Floridians, the story of Jose Padilla and his conversion to Islam should put every South Florida resident on high alert. Padilla was born in 1970 in a predominantly Hispanic neighborhood in Chicago. At a young age, Padilla joined a Puerto Rican street gang known as the "Latin Disciples" and was convicted of aggravated battery and armed robberies while still a juvenile. In the fall of 1991, at the age of 21, Jose Padilla and his family headed to Florida. It wasn't long until he found himself in a Broward County jail stemming from a road-rage incident in which he fired a pistol at another driver.

Upon his release, he got a job at Taco Bell. He was befriended by the manager of the Taco Bell—a Muslim-Pakistani immigrant, Mohammad Javed Qureshi, and co-founder of the *Sunrise School of Islamic Studies*. Having been exposed to radical Islam while in prison, Mohammad Qureshi built on the foundation established through the Muslim prison ministry. Padilla converted to Islam at a mosque in Sunrise, Florida, in 1994. At the time, the Imam at the mosque was Raed Awad, a fundraiser for the Holy Land Foundation for Relief and Development (HLF) in Florida.[75] On December 4, 2001, approximately three months after 9/11, HLF was placed in the category of "specially designated global terrorists," pursuant to Executive Order 12947.[76]

In 1998, Padilla moved to Egypt to learn Arabic and to deepen his understanding of Islam. He then moved to Pakistan, where, before September 11, 2001, Padilla met Zayn al-Abidin Mohammad Husayn Abu Zubaydah. Zubaydah was Osama bin-Laden's chief of military operations for Al-Qaeda. Padilla became Zubaydah's apprentice during 2001-2002 while Zubaydah was organizing the remnants of the Al-Qaeda network scattered by the U.S. attack on Afghanistan. Zubaydah was preparing a plan to detonate a radiological weapon or "dirty bomb" in the United States. (The TV series *24* is more real than you think.) In March 2002, Zubaydah sent Padilla to meet Al-Qaeda leaders and to work with an associate in order to make the bomb. Zubaydah was arrested a few weeks later and was turned over to U.S. authorities. Information obtained from Zubaydah led to Padilla's arrest at O'Hare International Airport after traveling from Pakistan to Zurich, then to Egypt, then back to Zurich, then on to Chicago. He was carrying more than ten thousand dollars in cash!

According to Zubaydah, Padilla had been sent back to the US to find radioactive material that could be used to build a dirty bomb.

Padilla now sits in Federal prison, but his life exemplifies the point. Exposed first to violent Islam while in prison, he was then recruited in the United States, trained abroad and finally returned to the United States as an Al-Qaeda terrorist, targeting his native country.

The foregoing story raises red flags on a number of different levels. The prison system was the incubator and petri dish for the growth of violent Islam within Jose Padilla. The fact that stories like Jose Padilla are not being told to the American people continues to allow the average American to wallow in our state of denial until it may be too late.

Padilla is an excellent example of what the Islamofascists look for within our United States—minority males, poor, uneducated, alienated, and a history of trouble with authority. Alone and vulnerable in prison, they are easily manipulated and swayed, first into conversion to Islam, and ultimately into the violence and death it preaches. There is an ample supply of men fitting this profile throughout America's prison system. There are 5.6 million Americans who are in prison or who have served time in prison. The National Islamic Prison Foundation claims to convert 135,000 prisoners every year. Even if only 10 percent of such converts subscribe to violence, the number is terrifying.

In light of these alarming statistics, the government—through the Office of Inspector General (OIG]) in April 2004—prepared a report entitled, "A Review of the Bureau of Prisons' Selection of Muslim Religious Services Providers." OIG identified significant problems related to the selection of Muslim religious service providers:

- The Bureau of Prisons (BOP) does not examine the doctrinal beliefs of applicants for religious service positions to determine whether those beliefs are consistent or inconsistent with BOP security policies;
- The BOP and FBI do not adequately exchange information regarding the BOP's endorsing organizations;

- Once contractors and certain volunteers gain access to the Bureau of Prisons facilities, ample opportunity exists for them to deliver extremist messages without supervision from BOP staff;
- BOP inmates frequently lead Islamic religious services with only minimal supervision from BOP staff members, enhancing the likelihood that seditious, treasonous or inappropriate content can be delivered to the inmates.[77]

When vetting potential Muslim chaplains, the BOP does not ask them whether they have received funds from foreign governments or whether they have spent time in a country that does not have diplomatic relations or treaties with the United States. In Ohio, an Ohio State Prisons Report concluded that conversion to Islam had led some inmates to become members of terrorist groups, including Hezbollah.[78]

At a time when we should be watching the prison system with greater scrutiny, the Islamofascists' unwitting collaborators, the ACLU is doing all it can to oppose the scrutiny.[79] Reprinted here is a warning from the OIG's report after a review of the "Federal Bureau of Prisons' Selection of Muslim Religious Services Providers:"

> The presence of extremist chaplains, contractors, or volunteers in the BOP's correctional facilities can pose a threat to institutional security and could implicate national security if inmates are encouraged to commit terrorist acts against the United States. For this reason, it is imperative that the BOP has in place sound screening and supervision practices that will identify persons that seek to disrupt the order of its institutions or to inflict harm on the United States through terrorism.[80]

American Naiveté

Historically, Americans have been, and, to a large extent still are, naïve when it comes to world affairs. The majority of Americans believe in the fundamental goodness of most people and, because most Americans are fundamentally good people themselves, they tend to view others, at least initially, with acceptance and trust. The vast majority of Americans are still largely uninformed about the threat we face. The silence of the mainstream media is deafening, and what little reporting that does take place is misleading. Political correctness and "tolerance" of our higher educational institutions blind our youth. The unwillingness of both the Bush and Obama administrations to identify or even acknowledge to the American people the existence of Islamic Supremacism lulls Americans into a false sense of security. Most citizens remain in the dark.

Ten years after...and still asleep

Some of our political leaders are beginning to rise up and ring the alarm bells. In 2007, the US House of Representatives and Senate organized caucuses on anti-terrorism. Congresswoman Sue Myrick from North Carolina has been, and is, a strong voice crying in the wilderness about the threat we face. More recently, Florida Congressman Allen West unabashedly shares historical truths about the violent history of Islam whenever it is appropriate to do so. Much more is needed, especially within the U.S. military. The Fort Hood massacre was preventable. The politically correct blindness to Islamic Jihad within their own ranks by Major Hassan's reviewers is criminal.

Ending American Naiveté

Every American needs to be informed. Knowledge is power, and awareness is the first step of self-defense. No treatment can begin for a disease until it is recognized and diagnosed. Similarly, no battle can be fought until the enemy is clearly identified. This is not a war on terror. Islam is not a traditional religion as we understand it. Islamic Supremacism is an ideology. Al Qaeda, Hezbollah, and Hamas all subscribe to the same ideology. We must stop allowing our political leaders and journalists to fail to identify, and inaccurately describe the war that America faces. As the Holy Land Foundation trial documents revealed, this is a war by a people bent on world domination and the establishment of a global caliphate. This is a war on Islamic Supremacism.

The main reason Americans continue to be naïve and uninformed about the Islamofascist threat is because our politicians and journalists, through the suicidal demands of political correctness, fail to accurately describe the war embroiling America. As Harvey Kushner eloquently stated, "Political correctness has made us so afraid of being branded racist that we force ourselves to be colorblind, identity-blind and gender-blind, until we end up, quite simply, totally blind."[81]

For the first time in about 200 years, America must come to grips with the fact that we are fighting a war on our own soil, on our own turf. The war is here; the war is now. Will we prevail?

Part 3
The Sheep, the Wolf, the Sheepdog and the Rescue of the Big Earth Ranch

Once upon a time there was this big old ranch.[82] This giant plot of land was called the "Big Earth Ranch" and was populated by many different creatures. But the Big Earth Ranch was run by only the most intelligent of the creatures: talking wolves, talking sheep and talking sheepdogs.

All three of the superior creatures were equal in intelligence. The difference between them was only in how they viewed one another.

Sheep were kind, decent animals not capable of hurting one another or wolves, or sheepdogs, unless by accident or unless under extreme provocation. In fact, if the Big Earth Ranch was populated by only sheep, well, the Ranch would be very peaceful. But, Big Earth Ranch had other intelligent creatures called wolves, and they were nothing like sheep. They especially liked to feed on the most defenseless of creatures, including sheep.

There was a lot of debate as to whether there were even wolves at all or why wolves acted the way they did. Most sheep preferred to go on about their business, ignoring the fact that wolves existed or even denying that they existed at all.

Sheep did understand there were dangers in the Big Earth Ranch, like fire and bad weather. So they supported fire alarms, firefighters and weathermen. But sheep could not handle the fact that there were other talking creatures that roamed the Big Earth Ranch that wished to harm them. Sheep were inflicted with the inherent inability to see other creatures on the Ranch for what they really were. They could only see them as sheep: peaceful and non-violent.

That is why there were sheepdogs. But for sheepdogs, sheep would have become extinct many generations ago. Sheepdogs were *born* to protect and defend the sheep. They *lived* to confront the wolf.

But there was a problem. Most sheep did not like sheepdogs. The sheepdog was a reminded that there were wolves on the Big Earth Ranch and sheep did not like to be that fact. It made them feel uncomfortable. They also didn't like the sheepdog because in order to protect the sheep, the sheepdog had to look and act a lot like a wolf. That made the sheep nervous. The sheep liked to pretend that wolves didn't even exist. They even fantasized that wolves and sheep could get along if they just talked things out, or, if sheep could better understand the root causes of the wolves' desire to kill sheep.

However, when the wolf did show up ready to eat them sheep would always rediscover how much they appreciated the sheepdog. The sheep from France were most like that. French sheep would say all kinds of bad things about the sheepdog until one day when the wolf marched through Paris. For a while, the French treated the sheepdogs like heroes. After the sheepdogs drove the wolves away they became heroes for a time. But when the danger passes, the sheepdog becomes unpopular again.

Within the Big Earth Ranch was the American Ranch, one of the largest spreads inside the Big Earth Ranch. On September 11, 2001, the wolves showed up inside the American Ranch. On that day the wolves killed a bunch of sheep. Sheepdogs became very popular for a while. Later, however, the sheep began complaining about the sheepdogs. Sheep have short memories. The wolves count on that. In the Europe Ranch, the sheep were in charge. The sheep of the Europe Ranch were willing to risk their lives and their entire Ranch on the proposition that sheep and wolves could live harmoniously together, forgetting and rewriting memories and history.

But the American Ranch was different. It was founded by sheepdogs, and was always a nation filled with sheepdogs. There were professional sheepdogs, amateur sheepdogs, mommy sheepdogs, daddy sheepdogs, and sheepdogs that, for generations, were imbued with an attitude that said, "If it's going to be, it's up to me." If his neighbor's house got blown away, he wouldn't wait for FEMA to show up to get help. He would get with other sheepdogs and … just get it done. Afterward, without fanfare, the sheepdog would go back to his own life.

There were sheepdogs on United Flight 93, and the mission of that homicide flight was defeated.

But over on the Europe Ranch, some time later, a terrible thing happened. Many sheepdogs on the Europe Ranch didn't like how the sheep treated them, so they went over to the American Ranch where they were appreciated. There weren't that many sheep left on the Europe Ranch to protect anyway. After that, the rest of the sheep disappeared. Some sheep got eaten by the wolves. Some sheep stopped having lambs and died off. That's when the Europe Ranch became filled with wolves and it became a very violent, unhappy place.

"What happened to the American Ranch?," the children wanted to know. That is the last chapter of the story and it is being written now. So, go thank an American sheepdog, while you still can, and maybe the story will have a happy ending.

Is that America still a nation of sheepdogs?

Ultimately, that will determine the answer.

Chapter Five

Tolerance Is Cultural Suicide When It's A One-Way Street

Dancing with the devil of destruction

Tolerance—Motherhood, apple pie, the American tradition of immigration assimilation. Who, other than unrepentant racists, would suggest that tolerance is not a good thing?

But as this concept has evolved and morphed over the last twenty years, it is time to re-examine whether "tolerance" has become a Trojan horse; making the true nature of something to allow it into our culture without objection—even though that something will eventually be used to destroy us.

To examine tolerance and the danger that its unthinking application poses to our way of life one must first look back, then weigh where we are today, and finally, project where the trends of tolerance are leading us.

The way we were and are

Think back to your school days. Remember "Christmas Vacation"? Somewhere along the line it changed into the gelded "Winter Break." This was a symbol of our tolerance for those who don't celebrate Christmas. Now, even many Christian Schools denote the two weeks off in late December and early January as "Winter Break."

There was a time when Christmas carols were routinely performed in our public schools. Now public schools no longer allow the children to sing Christmas songs that have overtly religious tones. Little surprise there. "Silent

Night" has been silenced. But, in many cases, all Christmas songs are banned altogether. Even "Rudolph the Red-Nosed Reindeer" has been blackballed in some schools. Culturally, the only reason the December vacation existed was to coincide with the celebration of the birth of Christ. Today, "tolerance" can't or won't acknowledge the cultural roots of the holiday. Very recently, some schools in the northeast have been labeling the two weeks of vacation in December the "Winter Solstice," reverting to the pagan holiday that existed around December 21, two thousand years ago. At one time your city hall was actually allowed to have "Christmas" decorations. But demands were made to remove from the public square any displays that might share the religious origin of the holiday season.

It was a generation ago, or less, when the ten days of vacation for students in March or April was denoted "Easter Vacation." With the help of Hollywood, Annette Funicello and Fort Lauderdale Beach, the tolerant crowd won a permanent victory in renaming Easter Vacation "Spring Break."

Any Catholic over the age of 50 can remember reciting the "Our Father" in school every day. Many of you remember the Ten Commandments adorning your school hallway. The prayer is silenced and the Ten Commandments have been removed. And now, at graduation time—in our zeal to show tolerance to all—no prayer can be uttered in thanks for the accomplishments of the graduating students. This is not without its affect on the student body. In fact, a student in an Arizona high school composed his own—and it possesses enough wisdom to achieve anthem status:

The New School Prayer
Now I sit me down in school
Where praying is against the rule
For this great nation under God
Finds mention of Him very odd.
If Scripture now the class recites,
It violates the Bill of Rights.
And anytime my head I bow
Becomes a Federal matter now.

Our hair can be purple, orange or green,
That's no offense; it's a freedom scene.
The law is specific, the law is precise:
Prayers spoken aloud are a serious vice.
For praying in a public hall
Might offend someone with no faith at all.
In silence alone we must meditate,
God's name is prohibited by the state.
We're allowed to cuss and dress like freaks,
And pierce our noses, tongues and cheeks.
They've outlawed guns, but *first* the Bible.
To quote the Good Book makes me liable.
We can elect a pregnant Senior Queen,
And the "unwed daddy," our Senior King.
It's "inappropriate" to teach right from wrong,
We're taught that such "judgments" do not belong.
We can get our condoms and birth controls,
Study witchcraft, vampires and totem poles.
But the Ten Commandments are not allowed,
No Word of God much reach this crowd.
It's scary here, I must confess,
When chaos reigns the school's a mess.
So, Lord, this silent plea I make:
Should I be shot; My soul please take!
Amen.[83]

Our Founding Fathers' documents establishing the birth of this country are replete with thanks to a higher power for His blessings and replete with requests to His power for guidance and deliverance for a nation conceived in liberty. In 2006, a federal judge in Kentucky actually entered an injunction forbidding high school students from praying at their graduation! The fact that the graduating seniors blatantly disobeyed the court mandate and recited the Lord's Prayer in unison at their graduation should be comfort to those who believe that we, as a nation, are not yet in the end stages of cultural suicide.

How many people have now succumbed to wishing everyone "Happy Holidays" so as to be tolerant of those that do not celebrate Christmas? When Americans forego "Merry Christmas," as though that term were offensive, tolerance becomes cultural suicide—especially in light of the fact that 85 percent of Americans still identify themselves as Christians. Indeed, cultural suicide is well on its way in America when "Merry Christmas" becomes politically incorrect.

Unfortunately, this quest for a utopian society based on the false notion of tolerance has percolated up and out of the schools and into our mainstream culture. Even worse, it has mutated into an *intolerance* of traditional sacredness. So-called art, funded with your tax dollars, pays for a picture of a crucifix in a jar of urine, entitled "Piss Christ," and is displayed to the public in the Brooklyn Museum of Art.

But reverse intolerance is manifested in much less offensive ways when, for example, Condoleezza Rice, the former Secretary of State of the United States was invited to be the commencement speaker at Boston College and was vehemently opposed by its faculty and students. But, Ward Churchill, a radical American hater and former professor from the University of Colorado, is welcomed at the same university. Tolerance is cultural suicide when it's a one-way street.

Political correctness changes the way news is reported

"Political Correctness" or "tolerance," so as not to offend Muslims, affects the way Islamic violence is reported. It is absurd and dangerous because the average American is lulled into a false sense of security. Remember the terrorists who seized a theater in Moscow in 2002 leading to the tragic deaths of many Russian innocents? They were Islamic terrorists. However, the *New York Times* referred to them as "separatists" and "guerillas."

Remember the young man from California, John Walker Lindh, who fought for the Taliban and was captured by US troops? Well, it turns out that he had actually changed his name in high school to Suleyman Al-Lindh. When he was captured by American forces he was known by the name of

Abdul Hameed. Although it had been years since he was John Walker, that was the only name the politically correct press used for him.

Remember the shoe bomber on the plane? The press called him "Richard Reid." However, the name he responded to when trying to bomb a plane full of civilians was Abdul Rahim. The French police identified him as Tariq Raga, yet the tolerant press only referred to him as Richard Reid.

Remember the Washington DC snipers? The elder sniper had converted to Islam 17 years earlier, changing his name to John Mohammad, and proclaiming himself a follower of Louis Farrakhan's Nation of Islam. CNN, however, initially reported his name as John Allan Williams and a "Gulf War Veteran."

When the 17 terrorists were arrested in Canada, the *New York Times* described them as "Southern Asians" rather than that they all belonged to the Nation of Islam—the real truth.

On October 22, 2006, in a report on anger and resentment still festering in French areas scarred by the riots of 2005, both the *New York Times* and the *Baltimore Sun* reported on an ambush on police in a Paris suburb. The *New York Times* reported the perpetrators as "unemployed, undereducated youths, mostly the offspring of Arab and African immigrants." The *Baltimore Sun* reported the truth: the rioting was by "Muslim immigrants from North Africa…."

The tolerant crowd should heed well this advice: *When in doubt about the proper orientation of your moral compass, point it away from the people that want to behead you.* Tolerance, it seems, has an evil twin—an inability to discern what *cannot* be tolerated. (Alas, the sheep refuse, or don't want to recognize, the presence of wolves.

The Way We Are Headed: The Judge and the Cross

Judge Stableman could not believe the headline in the New England Constitution, the last printed newspaper still published in his community: "Judge to be indicted for hate crime."

How had it come to this?, he thought to himself. His law school record was been stellar. He qualified for the Law Review, and upon graduation took a position as a highly paid associate at one of the more high-profile law firms in the state. After toiling for six years as an associate, he was made a fast-track partner. Shortly after becoming partner, though, he eschewed the opportunity for extraordinary wealth, and answered a higher calling to put on the black robe, stating he wanted to make a difference in the community he loved.

He began his judicial career as a gubernatorial appointee to the bench. He was able to use the connections from his law firm to wrangle an appointment over other more experienced, perhaps more-qualified lawyer applicants. He began his judicial career in the county court handling misdemeanors, traffic offenses and small-claims suits. He soon distinguished himself by his courtroom demeanor, quick wit and the ability to zero-in on issues.

After a few years, he was promoted to a higher trial court that dealt only with felony crimes and civil cases where more than $75,000 was at stake. He attended church regularly with his wife and two children. After eight years on the trial bench, everyone assumed it was only a matter of time before his elevation to an appellate court became a reality. And then, Christmas of 2020 came along. Of course, by 2020, what had traditionally been called the "Christmas" season was now referred to as the "Winter Solstice" holiday.

By 2020, Judge Stableman's wife, Pamela, wanted her two children to have a Winter Solstice season that was all about Christmas. She was raising the children as Christians but dutifully sent James and Heather to public school so that they would have the chance to experience other students with diverse cultures, backgrounds and religious beliefs. Now that they were getting older, however, she was concerned that the children were completely forgetting "the reason for the season." Public schools had long since jettisoned the singing of Christmas songs years before it was determined that even songs like "Grandma Got Run Over By a Reindeer" might remind children of the Christmas holiday, which could be deemed offensive to atheists or other non-Christian religions.

So this year, Pamela decided to decorate the house differently. She kept the plastic Santa and the plastic Frosty the Snowman in the attic. She made a trip in early December to the nearest Christian Supply Center in order to purchase "Christmas" holiday decorations. The trip was an ordeal. She would have to drive 45 minutes each way. It took a long time and much money to choose and purchase just the right decorations. Three years before, when the local Wal-Mart, Target and JC Penney stores stopped carrying traditional Christmas decorations, she was in agreement with the other members of the PTA who thought it was a good idea. Muslims had begun to boycott the stores for carrying such items. Pamela Stableman understood how a Muslim walking into a store filled with Christmas displays might feel hurt and offended.

Thirty minutes into her trip, strange emotions welled up inside. Pamela began to resent Wal-Mart and the Muslims, whom she now blamed for causing her to make this 90-minute trip during a time of the year that was busy with *so* much to do. As she was driving, she thought about the Solstice celebration she had promised to attend and the Solstice cookies she had promised to bake for the party. The traffic was worse than she anticipated and now it looked like she would not get the cookies baked. Mrs. Stableman fretted over arriving at the party empty-handed. She dismissed her feelings as racist, and concluded the trip was worth it. After all, both Heather and James needed to see how front lawns *used* to be decorated when she was a little girl.

Pamela hadn't really discussed the project with her husband, but she was confident he would agree it was a good idea, even though he was a judge. She knew her husband was very sensitive to diverse peoples and cultures. He had made a point many times of not going forward with court hearings or trials when dealing with defendants or litigants whose first language was not English. One time he had even delayed a trial for months so that the public defender could obtain, at state expense, an interpreter for an Afghani from the northeast region of that country who spoke a unique dialect of Pashto.

When Mrs. Stableman finally arrived at the "Christmas" store, the inventory and displays took her breath away. Happy memories of her childhood flooded back. In her mind's eye she saw her mom and grandma laughing like schoolgirls as they shopped for extra knick-knacks so the house would be "just so." "Don't leave the 'Christ' out of Christmas," her mother would say. She fought back tears, and then became embarrassed when the sales clerk approached. Noticing that her teary eyes caught the clerk's attention, Pamela apologized.

"I'm sorry. It's just that …"

"Oh, don't even think about that," said the clerk kindly, "Almost everyone that comes in here these days gets all sentimental, remembering how it used to be."

The nice clerk helped Mrs. Stableman pack the car so the Christmas decorations would not jostle during the long ride back to New Canaan. Driving into her neighborhood, Pamela was most pleased with herself. She had bought a stable containing a solar light sensor that would illuminate the barn automatically after dark. The scene included some stable animals, Mary, Joseph and the manger containing Jesus. She had found a star that was attached to a long titanium pole. Once assembled, the brightly lit star would hover thirty feet over the manger scene and be visible throughout the neighborhood! At the last minute, Pamela also decided to buy something she knew no other house would display. It was not very common when she was a child, but Pamela thought in 2020 it was sorely needed. Mrs. Stableman had purchased a plain white 8-by-6 foot cross that would also illuminate at night. Because they were going to have "Christmas" decorations this year, she thought they might as well go all the way. As Pamela pulled into her driveway on that snowy afternoon, she could hardly contain her exuberance, and it became contagious. Both Heather and James liked the idea of having a unique Solstice display in their front yard. All three knew that not one house in the area would be decorated like theirs. They were all in the process of assembling the scene when Judge Stableman came home.

"What do we have here?" he asked, when he noticed that the faded Santa Claus and carrot-nosed Frosty the Snowman lying face down in the yard.

Pamela responded quickly, a little surprised that her tone became defensive. "Well, this year, honey, I decided we would have real 'Christmas' decorations. The kids are getting older and other than once a year in church, they have never really experienced 'Christmas.' So I got the stable, the manger, Mary and Joseph and, once this cross is assembled it's going to be eight feet high! And the star that the three wise men followed—well, people are going to be able to see that for blocks, maybe miles away!"

"Well, that sounds pretty cool," responded Judge Stableman.

The kids rolled their eyeballs. "Why does Dad use such old-fashioned expressions? Nobody says 'cool' anymore."

Judge Stableman went inside with his briefcase full of work. Pamela and the children finished the display. When it was done, it was a sight to behold.

None of the neighbors could remember the last time someone had a manger scene in their front yard for the Winter Solstice season. The star *was* actually visible for miles. The light from the cross illuminated the entire front yard and even brought light to the dark house next door. It wasn't long before word spread. Night after night cars would drive by, just to get a glimpse of the display. Despite the cold weather and occasional snow, many folks actually parked and got out of their cars, just to gaze at the awesome display.

On some nights when Pamela wasn't that busy, she would come out to chat with a few of what her kids called "the gawkers." Pamela could not help but notice the tears that welled up in the eyes of many as they marveled at the scene. Always busy with work he took home from the courthouse, Judge Stableman seemed oblivious to the newfound commotion on 1953 Elm Street in New Canaan, Connecticut.

Then, one night, two days before Christmas, but two days after the Winter Solstice Holiday, inside the Stableman house the phone rang. Pamela and the children were outside talking to the "gawkers" so Judge Stableman, alone in his study, answered the phone.

"Hello?"

"This is Joe Mumford." Joe was a political insider who had helped Judge Stableman get his appointment as a county court judge from the governor's office and, later, his appointment to the circuit court.

"Oh. Hi Joe. How are you?"

"I'm okay, but you're not. Your Solstice display is causing quite a commotion." "Why is that, Joe?"

"Crap, Judge, don't you know that you have Muslims that live right next door?"

"Yeah, so?"

"What do you mean, 'yeah, so'? Your star and cross are driving them nuts. They don't celebrate Christmas, and your display is like shoving it right down their throats. You are totally in their face."

"Aw, Joe, you're overreacting. I know Mr. Mamoud. We've always gotten along great. Whenever the hedge between our houses gets too high, he pays for the hedge-trimmer guy one year and I pay for him the next. Just because he doesn't celebrate Christmas, what's the big deal?"

"Judge, I think you've been out of politics too long. They filed a complaint with the American Civil Liberties Union, and the ACLU has asked for a criminal investigation."

"A criminal investigation? What are you talking about?"

"What I'm talking about, Judge, is a hate crime. You, more than anybody else, ought to know what a hate crime is. You can't do anything that might offend somebody who doesn't have the same beliefs as you. Listen, Judge, I know you're on the civil side of the courthouse right now but you used to be on the criminal side. You need to be aware that your display is considered intolerant and offensive."

"Joe, when I presided on the criminal side the hate crime legislation hadn't been passed yet."

"Well, Judge, you need to pay attention, because one, you have Muslims that live next door; two, you have a display on your front yard that is overtly Christian; and three, you should know that any overtly Christian display on your front yard is going to offend your non-Christian next door neighbor. That's a hate crime, Judge."

"Well, Joe, I appreciate your concern, but I think you're overreacting. Don't forget, five years ago I received the 'Jurist of the Year' award from the Muslim-American Relations Foundation when I insisted that there be Arabic translators in the courthouse for all criminal proceedings. Besides, Mamoud is a good guy, and I don't see any problem. Good-bye, Joe. And by the way, Merry Christmas."

"Geez, Judge, take it easy with that stuff, will you? I think you need to take down the display and issue a formal apology."

"Joe, let me talk to Pamela. I'll get back to you."

The Judge walked outside to talk to Pamela. As he walked up to the manger scene, a family who had just parked their car got out. It was a mother and father with their three kids. The Judge didn't recognize them. He was approached by the father, who then waved for his family to follow as he came forward.

"Hey, you're Judge Stableman, aren't you? Well I just want you to know, Judge, this is the greatest Christmas display I've seen in a long time. My kids go to school down at Apple Blossom Elementary, and when I heard about your display I had to bring them by. Nobody has displays like this anymore, Judge, and I just want you to know… you're my hero."

The Judge mumbled a "thank you," but was completely taken aback by the father's appreciation. His initial thought was, "What is this guy talking about? I'm no hero."

The man corralled his family back into the car, rolled down his window and as he drove away said, "Keep it up, Judge, you're the best." Judge Stableman's thoughts did not dwell on the nice man.

"Pam, I just received a phone call from Joe. He's concerned about our display."

"Honey," his wife responded, "We've received more compliments about this display than you can possibly imagine! Heather and James are all the rage at their school and they've been asked to give talks in their civics class about free speech…whatever that's about."

"But Pam, Joe seems concerned that we might be offending the Mamouds with this display."

"For having a manger scene in our front yard?" Pamela asked. "Oh, come on, sweetie, you know Joe, he always overreacts. Political consultants are too cautious."

Judge Stableman walked away. His wife's common sense was convincing. He decided not to call Joe back.

The whole thing had died down by February 2021. Then the phone call came. It was Friday, before Presidents' weekend. It was Joe.

"Judge, you didn't listen to me. I told you, but you didn't listen to me!"

"What, Joe, what?"

"You're going to be indicted, Judge. And the Judicial Qualifications Commission is going to look into your fitness to continue to be a judge."

"What are you talking about, Joe?"

"Judge, the holiday display, remember? You have the whole Muslim community in New Canaan outraged. Now they even want to have the name of the town changed, since "Canaan" is a biblical name. I don't know if I can help you on this one. The political damage is too great. I think in order to protect the governor you're going to have to resign…"

The newspaper arrived the next morning…

It's more real than you think

Can the made-up story of Judge Stableman really happen here? When Condoleeza Rice was Secretary of State pioneering that office as the first black woman to hold the position, she was picketed, spat upon and even discouraged from appearing on numerous college campuses around the United States based on her political views. So much for tolerance and the free exchange of ideas at institutions of "higher" learning.

Abraham Lincoln once said, "The philosophy of the schoolroom in one generation becomes the philosophy of the government in the next."[84]

Michelle Shocks of Seattle was riding home on a bus one day when another passenger boarded, saying, "Praise the Lord!" The boarding bus rider was happy to be out of the pouring rain. The two started to privately discuss religion across the aisle. The bus driver could overhear them, however, and ordered them to stop their discussion because it might "offend" other passengers. Michelle moved to a seat next to the recently boarded passenger and they continued their discussion in hushed tones. The driver pulled to the side of the road and demanded that both passengers leave the bus. Michelle, who was 25 years old and five months pregnant, was forced to *walk* the last mile to her home, in the rain.[85]

The American Bar Association proposed a change to its ethics rules in August of 2004, suggesting that judicial candidates and judges be forced to quit groups like the Boy Scouts or be removed from the bench. The Boy Scouts, you ask? Yes, because the Scouts were deemed to be intolerant by refusing to allow homosexuals to be scoutmasters.[86]

The law is changing before our eyes. Slowly, and insidiously, our freedoms are being taken away. A radical assault on American values has taken place over the last 40 years. It has gone largely unreported in the mainstream media.

Below is a brief survey of recent Supreme Court decisions that have changed our country and our traditional American values. After reading what follows, ask yourself if the story you just read is not far off.

Verbal prayer in our public schools has been declared unconstitutional, even if that prayer is both voluntary and denominationally neutral. See *Engle v. Vitale,* 370 U.S. 421, (1962); *Abington v. Schempp*, 374 U.S. 203, (1963).

In *Reed v. Van Hoven,* 237 F. Supp. 48, (W. D. Mich., 1965), it was decided that if a student prays over his lunch it is unconstitutional for him to pray out loud. When a student in a public school addresses an assembly of his peers he effectively becomes a government representative and it is therefore unconstitutional for that student to engage in prayer. See *Harris v. Joint School District,* 41 F.3rd 447, (9th Cir., 1994).

In 1999, in the case of *Rubin v. City of Burbank,* 101 Cal. App. 4th 1194 (2002), the court decided that a city council meeting can offer prayer, so long as the council does not offer the name of Jesus.

In *Gierke v. Blotzer,* CV-88-0-883, USDC Neb., 1989, a student in Omaha, Nebraska was prohibited from reading his Bible *silently* during study hall and was even enjoined from *opening* his Bible at school.

The case of *Roberts v. Madigan,* 921 F. 2nd 1047, (10th Circuit, 1990) declared it to be unconstitutional for a classroom library to contain books that deal with Christianity or for a teacher to be seen with a personal copy of his or her Bible at school.

With regard to crosses, it has been declared unconstitutional for a public cemetery to have a planter in the shape of a cross, for if someone were to view that cross, such viewing could cause emotional distress and injury. *Warsaw v. Tehachapi,* CV-F-90-404 USDC, E. D. Cal, 1990.

In June 2004, the Los Angeles County Supervisors voted 3-2 to remove a tiny cross from the official county seal rather than face a potential lawsuit from the ACLU. The cross had been on the county seal for 47 years!

On September 22, 2004, under California Law SB1234, individuals can now claim that someone expressing their deeply held religious beliefs present an "intimidating threat."[87]

Canada recently passed a hate crimes law which has been dubbed the "Bible as hate literature bill." It makes public criticism of homosexuality a crime.[88]

As Judeo-Christianity is forced out of the public square, the spiritual vacuum created is rapidly being filled—by Sharia-compliant laws and regulations.

Footbaths are being installed on many college campuses. Noise ordinances in Dearborn, Michigan and surrounding communities are being modified so as to "accommodate" the five-times daily Muslim call to prayer. Ramadan fasting is now accommodated in workplaces and a poultry processing plan in Arkansas was asked to delete the Labor Day holiday in place of a Muslim religious holiday. A judge in Tampa, Florida recently allowed Sharia law to apply to a domestic relations family law case. Since Sharia law also permits honor killings and stoning, where is the line to be drawn once the descent down the slippery slope of Sharia law begins?

Ask yourself this question: Is the indictment of Judge Stableman all that unrealistic?

Tolerance is cultural suicide when it is a one-way street.

Chapter Six
Will Judeo-Christianity Survive?

"Upon this rock I shall build this church, and the gates of Hell shall
not prevail against it"

It seems everywhere Islam goes, violence follows. Violence continues to rage in Afghanistan as the Taliban intensify their aggression against Americans, their own countrymen and fellow Muslims. In December 2006, the Taliban were murdering teachers—mostly young women—as collaborators in the new government, the participants of which are branded as infidels. In Iran, where there is a particularly virulent form of Sharia-compliant Islam, the mullahs race ahead on a collision course with Israel and the United States over nuclear weapons. In July 2006, Somalia's top Islamic leader called for a holy war against Ethiopia to drive out troops the largely Christian nation of Ethiopia sent to protect the internationally-backed Somali government. In Lebanon, Hezbollah and Hamas fight each other, Israelis, Americans, and the West. In Iraq, both Shiite and Sunni mosques suffer attacks from bombs and mortars.

When the Islamic radicals—and let's no longer dignify them as "insurgents"—are not killing each other, they are targeting Americans or any "infidel" that wants to bring democracy to the country in question. In Sri Lanka, government troops clash with Tamil tiger "rebels." The rebels are radical Islamists. In Pakistan, a suicide bomber blows himself up outside the home of a prominent Shiite Muslim cleric, triggering a riot in Karachi. In India, bombers attack Bombay's rail system killing thousands. Islamic violence increases daily in that Hindu country. In Nigeria, Islamic forces kill Christians on sight. In the Darfur region of the Sudan, ethnic cleansing is ongoing and South Sudan has seceded, unable to peacefully co-exist with their Muslim "brothers" to the North. Egypt convulses in revolution, as does Tunisia. Libya is in the throes of a civil war as violence simultaneously erupts in Syria, Yemen and Algeria. Chechnya "rebels" in Russia kill women and children. The "rebels" are Islamic fascists, despite the fact that the news media refuses to identify them as such. Islamic fascists blow up trains in Spain, riot in France, blow up busses and trains in London and are caught in Canada before having the opportunity to do the same. The news media asks, "Why Canada?" The Canadian government has not supported the United States in its war in Afghanistan or Iraq. Canada has a very open-door immigration policy towards Muslims. So why Canada? Those who ask that question don't get it.

Former Senator Rick Santorum does get it. In a speech delivered on July 20, 2006, he stated, "The biggest issue facing our children's future is a war. Not as so many describe it, the War on Terror. Not the war in Iraq or Afghanistan. But the world war which, at its heart, is just like the previous three global struggles."[89]

The Senator is referring to the war with Islamic Supremacists.

In World War II the United States and other freedom-loving countries fought German Nazis and Japanese imperialists. Today, the threat to freedom is from Islamic Supremacists. Consider the citizens of Australia, Indonesia, Thailand, Lebanon and Argentina. Those countries have also suffered firsthand and mourned innocent victims as a result of terrorism at the hands of Islamic Supremacists. What hostile foreign policy in Thailand caused the radical Islamists to attack the government there?

Ronald Reagan branded communism as an "Evil Empire" and, although criticized for it, he was right. All enlightened people understood that Nazism was an evil regime. We must understand with moral clarity this war against Islamic Supremacists. Our failure to appreciate the danger entails the ultimate price: that western value of individual freedom and human dignity will not survive.

The Islamic Messiah

Islam's aggression into the West began during the period of what westerners were taught as the "Dark Ages." The first period of Islamic aggression began in the 7th century. Islamic expansion continued virtually unabated for centuries. The Ottoman Empire ruled from the western border of India on the east, to the gates of Vienna to the west. The end of World War I brought the demise of the Ottoman Empire. Sixty years later, In 1979, as radicals deposed the Shah of Iran, the modern era of Islamic Supremacy and expansion began. The new leaders of Iran called the United States "the Great Satan" and promised to destroy Israel. Over 30 years have passed and the vitriol towards all things western not only continues, but intensifies.

In a November 16, 2005 speech in Tehran to senior clerics who had come from all over Iran to hear him, Ahmadinejad, the president of Iran, stated that the main mission of his government was to "pave the way for the glorious reappearance of Imam Mahdi, may God hasten his reappearance."[90] The mystical Twelfth Imam of Sh'ia Islam is venerated by many in Iran. Who is the Twelfth Imam, known as "the Mahdi"? Islamic end-times prophecy calls for the appearance of a messiah who is called "the Lord of the Age" or "the Awaited Savior." According to Islamic teaching, he disappeared as a child in 941 C.E. and Sh'ia Muslims have been awaiting his reappearance ever since. They believe that when he returns he will reign on earth for seven years, bringing about the last judgment and the end of the world as we know it. What should concern all non-Muslims is that his reign is preceded by a *worldwide conflict*—the Muslim version of the battle of Armageddon.

In September 2005, Ahmadinejad finished his U.N. speech with a prayer for the imminent coming of the Mahdi, whom he called "a perfect human being who is heir to all prophets and pious men." The Ahmadinejad cabinet has allocated $17 million to renovate the Jamkarin mosque, where devotees of the Twelfth Imam have come to pray for centuries. Ahmadinejad has told regime officials that the Mahdi will reappear in a few years. Devotees of the Twelfth Imam believe that only increased violence, conflict and oppression will bring about the Mahdi's return. Since assuming power in Iran, Ahmadinejad has placed Twelfth Imam devotees in his cabinet and throughout the bureaucracy.

Concurrently, Ahmadinejad is moving aggressively to stop the proliferation of Christian home churches throughout the country.

He has stated, "I will stop Christianity in this country."

Meanwhile, Iran continues to defy the United Nations as it proceeds unabated in its quest for nuclear capability. A religious zealot with nuclear weapons, vowing to destroy Israel and the United States, and believing that he will usher in the Twelfth Imam and his accompanying worldwide conflict is a dangerous witches brew. Will America survive?

The Islamic States of America[91]*– circa 2021*

The U.N. General Assembly rose in unison to applaud the announcement by the ambassador to the U.N. from the Islamic States of America (I.S.A.) that the "Bible Belt Rebellion"—as the uprising had been dubbed—was finally subdued after three years of violence. The I.S.A.'s ambassador to the United Nations gave a brief history of the conflict when he made his announcement.

"In 2017, we expected more tolerance from the radical Christian groups that formerly controlled parts of Louisiana, Mississippi, Alabama, Georgia, North Florida, the Carolinas, Tennessee, Arkansas and West Virginia. When those states refused to accept the mandatory Sharia compliant curriculum made necessary because Islam was ignored for 250 years in the public schools, we were patient for a time. But after they rebelled against the National School Dress Code, enacted out of sensitivity to Sharia-compliant students, we had no choice but to send in federal marshals."

U.S. Marshals were deployed to quell the riots blamed on "Christian Extremists". The new National Dress Code for all public schools required that *all* girls cover their faces, out of sensitivity for Sharia-compliant female students who are required to do so under Sharia law. When the marshals showed up to enforce the new "enlightened" policy, a clearly organized rebellion attacked and killed the marshals throughout the region.

The ambassador continued his report to the General Assembly: "The intolerant Christians hid for years in the Appalachian Mountains. Yesterday, we captured and killed the leader of the rebellion, Christian Cromwell.

His militia surrendered soon after. It could have been worse. Thankfully the I.S.A. had signed the United Nations Gun Ban Treaty years before. The citizen rebellion, unable to re-arm, ran out of ammunition and replacement parts for their guns."

The applause that swept the General Assembly, now located in Copenhagen—the capital of the Eurabia Union—was deafening.

The Islamic States of America Ambassador continued, "In accordance with International Law, we will seek the death penalty for all involved. We would like the beheadings of those responsible to serve as an example to all intolerant Christians that no disobedience to our duly-elected Caliphate will be sanctioned."

Many in the audience remembered the United States of America before it became the Islamic States of America. About 13 years before, the world was fed up with America's intolerant, warlike foreign policy. The Zionist-Christian warlords in America believed they were invincible. But with the election of 2008, everything changed. The electorate had finally voted the aggressors out of office. The new President, Barack Hussein Obama, promising hope and change, began to radically reshape America's foreign and domestic policy. His Department of Homeland Security published a national security memo warning all law enforcement agencies to be on the lookout for radicalized right-wing extremists. Police were warned that returning veterans could be prone to violence. Pro-life groups, anti-gun control citizens, as well as those that opposed America's open border immigration policies could pose a danger to America's security, the report said. The nation became polarized on ideological grounds. Those in disagreement with the new administration's policies were deemed enemies of the state.

In foreign policy, the Pentagon, seeing which way the political winds were blowing, banned use of the words "Jihad," "radical Islam," or "Islamafascists" in its daily briefings and official documents. The "War on Terror" was discarded for the more politically correct "Overseas Contingency Operation."

The new president gave his *first* television Interview, not on American television but on the television voice of all Muslims, Al-Jazeera. He made his *first* overseas state visit to a Muslim country. He reached out to the President of Iran and hugged Hugo Chavez, while accepting Chavez's gift of a book outlining the western world's alleged history of five hundred years of oppression of minorities.

The American people fell deeper into their slumber, ignoring the wolves at the door. Radical Islam prepared for war. After his re-election in 2012, the president emboldened by his re-election, announced plans to withdraw all troops in any locations which were deemed hostile to the Muslim community. It was now commonly believed that Muslim violence against America was simply the result of American military presence in Muslim countries. The prevailing thought, especially in the State Department, was that only after the withdrawal of American troops from Islamic countries could relations with these nations improve. Iranian President Mahmoud Ahmadinejad praised the president for his clear vision and sound judgment. Americans rejoiced as Obama convinced them he had brought peace with honor to the United States. Obama was lauded by the press for restoring America's respect abroad. On September 30, 2013, the last C5A Galaxy carrying the last company of combat troops left a small oil-rich country in the Middle East.

By December 6, 2013, it had been almost one year since the Democrat Party had regained control of Congress and kept the White House for a second consecutive term. President Obama was awarded his 2nd Nobel Peace Prize.

Americans had become supremely confident in their exercise of good judgment in electing new leaders espousing peace. Most Americans were proud of their government again, convinced of the importance of America being respected as a world citizen. "We're all citizens of the world" was the slogan that united the voters and launched Obama into his second term.

Americans had long since forgotten the report by the *New York Times* on March 31, 2007. Six years earlier the *Times* had reported that the U.S. Inspector General's office, the government agency in charge of safeguarding America's technical secrets about nuclear weapons, declared that it was missing twenty desktop computers. In fact, it was the *thirteenth* time in four years that an audit found the department, whose national laboratories and factories did most of the work in designing and building nuclear warheads, had lost control of the computers containing the design information on small, tactical nuclear bombs. Nobody seemed overly concerned. The Occupy Wall Street sit-ins and peace demonstrations overshadowed any concern for national security.

It took the thieves about six years to perfect the designs and delivery system plans outlined in the stolen computers. Late in the evening of December 6, 2013, a junior analyst in the National Security Agency was reviewing routine satellite images of ship movements in the Atlantic and Pacific within five hundred miles of the American coast.[92] The analyst thought he saw something unusual in the photos and called his supervisor at home. "Boss, I am emailing you photos of vessels I have been watching."

He continued, "Look at the boats. They look like fishing trawlers or private yachts. They've been moving in along shipping lanes for several days, across the Pacific toward the West Coast, and up from South America toward the East Coast. They are all small and slow, but if you look at the times and courses, it appears that they will all approach our coastline at about the same time and will all be about the same distance off our shores."

The supervisor, upset at being disturbed at home about fishing trawlers, dismissed him, "They're fishing boats. Don't worry about it."

At 2:00 p.m. on December 7, 2013, the first of four nuclear electromagnetic pulse devices, or EMPs, hit the Washington, D.C. area exploding about five hundred feet above the White House. Four other missiles reached their destinations shortly thereafter: one over the Pentagon; one over the U.S. Capitol; and one over F.B.I. headquarters. In a matter of minutes, all electronic devices serving two million people in the greater Washington, DC, area were fried or rendered inoperable. All cell phones were silenced. Cars halted en-route. Trains, planes and electricity all ceased. Without communication or electricity, the United States government was decapitated. At about the same time, missiles exploded over the New York Stock Exchange, the financial district of Boston, the Norfolk, Virginia Naval Base and Baltimore Harbor. All electricity ceased from Virginia to Massachusetts.

On the West Coast, the same type of short-range nuclear EMP devices exploded over Los Angeles, and the Silicon Valley of Santa Clara County. The northwest coastal cities were not overlooked. Portland, Oregon and Seattle, Washington lost all power and communication when the electromagnetic pulse fried every circuit board within 100 miles including the headquarters of Microsoft, Intel and Dell Computers.

The missiles were less than twenty feet long and only eighteen inches in diameter. They were powered by small, fuel-efficient, high-octane turbo fans painted in light blue and light gray, flying at a low altitude to avoid detection. They were state-of-the-art designs six years before. In January 2007, the Administrator of the National Nuclear Security Agency had been fired because of the theft scandals, but now six years later, it became apparent the action was too little and too late.

The attacks came from fishing trawlers using launch tubes that could be dismantled and stored in the holds under ice and fish. The platform prototype had been tested and used extensively by Hamas and Hezbollah in 2006 and 2007 in rockets launched from the Gaza strip and Lebanon into Israel. By 2013, the launch platform had been perfected and the nuclear capability of the electronic magnetic pulse bomb was operational. Iran's nuclear research which had continued unabated for a decade, was now bearing results.

As soon as each trawler launched its pair of missiles, the crew abandoned ship and quickly moved into rubber inflatable boats. As the last man climbed over the side, a timer was started on the explosive devices rigged in the bilge of each trawler. Thirty minutes later and five miles away, as each crewmember was climbing up the net on the side of a small freighter of Liberian registry, the charges placed in the bilges of each of the fishing trawlers exploded, sending any evidence of the attacks to the bottom of the ocean. Each terrorist was issued new identification as the ship's crew. The rubber inflatables that carried them there were shot and sunk.

With no obvious enemy to blame, and with discourse on radical Islam having been forbidden, fingers pointed in every direction. With no electricity or communications network, by Christmas 2013, the American economy was destroyed. Inflation, already high because of the wild spending sprees of 2009 and 2010 to "stimulate the economy," now soared completely out of control as the dollar collapsed and the U.S. Treasury printed money to meet its obligations without sufficient economic output to back the issuance of the currency. Unemployment spiked as major centers of employment grinded to a halt by the EMPs. Businesses closed by the thousands. Tax revenues evaporated, so state governments had no funds to pay unemployment benefits or teachers' salaries. For the first time in U.S. history, both the state and federal governments defaulted on their bond obligations. China and oil-rich, middle east nations called their loans.

With the New York Stock Exchange without power, stock trading came to a halt. Stock values plummeted. Retirement assets and pension funds, already battered by the 2008-2009 recession, disappeared virtually overnight. Without electricity, cities were in complete chaos in January, 2014. The residential real estate market, still reeling from the Fannie Mae and Freddie Mac meltdown, now looked good in comparison to the commercial real estate crash. Major banks filed for bankruptcy. But this time the Government had no money to bail them out. Riots erupted everywhere as panic set in. Faced with such large scale devastation, most Americans welcomed his absolute power.

With the collapse of the American economy, which was the largest on earth and responsible for producing one-third of world's economic output, it wasn't long before the rest of the global economy fell into chaos as well. Oil deliveries stopped, food shipments ceased and millions of people began to starve throughout the world.

Amidst the chaos, the president declared Marshall Law, assumed control of what was left of the American government and immediately consolidated his power. Barack Hussein Obama, having been the first president of Muslim descent elected to office, now became the supreme ruler of the United States by default.

Taking advantage of the chaos in America and the political cowardice of the European officials, Muslim leaders in Europe seized upon the situation. Because one-third of all the babies being born in Europe by 2013 were of Muslim descent, Muslim clerics demanded more representation in the parliaments throughout the continent and control of the European Union. Chaos reigned. The great riots of 2006 that took place in France were repeated in 2013, except this time, all of Western Europe erupted. The prophesy of worldwide chaos, necessary to usher in the Islamic Messiah had arrived. Faced with economic collapse, the European established order capitulated.

Muslim leaders assumed control of the government, the educational institutions and the press. Majority memberships on the boards of European banks and trading companies, mining companies and auto manufacturers soon followed. Sharia law prohibited the collection of interest on loans. As such, Muslim clerics demanded that of the World Bank and creditor nations, "Abolish interest charges and institute Sharia Law. The International Monetary Fund had no choice but to go along. Almost overnight the economic, social and political order of Europe was transformed.

As the chaos and riots escalated, people throughout Europe, the United States and Africa clamored for a leader that espoused peace, unity and no more violence. In the face of this global strife and chaos, the Grand Ayatollah of Iran stepped forward, calling for peace and an end to the senseless violence.

With the collapse of Iraq after the exit of U.S. troops in 2011, Iran had become the dominant player in the Middle East. First, the mullahs took control of the Iraqi oil fields. With America in chaos, the Saudi oil fields were next. The Sh'ia clerics based in Iran now called the shots for their satellite countries of Egypt (Mubarak having been deposed in 2011), Syria, Lebanon, Jordan, Iraq, Afghanistan, Saudi Arabia, Yemen, Ethiopia, Somalia, Tunisia, Sudan, and finally Libya, with the fall of Khadafy in 2011. Shia Iran now controlled 80% of the world's oil supply being brought to market. North America had the most proven reserves but it sat untapped, bottled up by environmental regulations, the EPA and a complicit Obama administration bent on enforcing its dream of ending America's reliance on fossil fuels for its energy.

Muslim leaders declared that Muslim prophecy had been fulfilled. The unrest of 2011 and 2012 helped to "pave the path for the glorious reappearance of Imam Mahdi." The mystical Twelfth Imam of Sh'ia Islam, whose glorious return had been anticipated for more than one thousand years, was now ready to appear. Sharia-compliant Muslims traveled to the United Nations in Copenhagen, where it had been hastily located after its headquarters was heavily damaged when the EMP exploded over Manhattan. When the Iranian Ayatollah introduced the Twelfth Imam to the United Nations, he suddenly felt, "surrounded by light." A "light from heaven," he claimed.

Later, it was reported that when the Mahdi began his speech in the name of "Allah," those present saw a light surround him, protecting him throughout his speech.

The mainstream press was in awe. The *New York Times* reported, "Suddenly the atmosphere changed, and for the thirty minutes of his talk, the leaders assembled before him could not blink. All of the leaders sat motionless, as if a hand held them and made them sit up and listen. They all had their eyes, ears and hearts open for the message from Allah and from the great Islamic prophet"

On January 21, 2014, the Mahdi took the stage at the United Nations and indicated that he would reign on the earth for seven years as the "Messiah", bringing about the last judgment upon all the infidels and upon all those who refused to convert to the last great religion, Islam. The U.S. president was there to welcome him.

All of the worlds' populace was called upon to begin the conversion process to Islam or face the consequences. The American president, Barack Hussein Obama, readily agreed. Most of the American people, facing unemployment, chaos, starvation and the end of life as they had known it, went along. After voting for a president who reminded them throughout two presidential campaigns and after his elections that they were all citizens of the world, that America was no longer a Christian nation, and that it was time to break down walls between all nations, all peoples and all religions, it seemed almost pre-ordained. Only one group resisted. For seven years, the constitutionalists, the Tea Party, the 9/12-ers and the fundamentalist Christians fought the onslaught of Sharia law. Slowly, each group was co-opted.

By 2017, the last holdouts were the intolerant Christians of the old American South. That's when open warfare broke out throughout the region, but, by 2020, the Christian rebellion had finally been put down and the world was now safe for Islam. Those that refused to accept Islam were either beheaded or forced into servitude working as second-class citizens, known as *dhimmitude*. After the defeat of the Christian rebellion in 2039—and because the rebellion had been so difficult to defeat--in 2021 the United Nations passed a binding resolution. All Muslims were to be branded with a mark so that non-Muslims could be easily distinguished. It was the natural next step of a policy that had begun in Iran in 2014. Then, all Jews in Iran were forced to again wear yellow stars so that they could be easily identified, and all Christians were forced to wear red stars so that they could be easily identified. Back then, the world yawned, and the policy was enacted. Now, in 2021, Christians throughout the world would not go undetected. Anyone without the mark of the Muslim would accept branding or get beheaded. The new underground Christian Internet blogs declared the Muslim "brand" was actually the mark of the beast as foretold in the Book of Revelation from the Christian Bible. Most people, however, scoffed at that notion. After all, hadn't the Mahdi brought peace to the world? As thousands were beheaded for refusing to accept the "Mark of World Patriotism," the irony of the new "peace" went unnoticed. The Judeo-Christian era was over. Planet Earth began a descent into a long, dark night, or did it?.

Wake Up Western Civilization!

Mark Steyn writes, "Permanence is the illusion of every age. In 1913, no one thought the Russian, Austrian, German and Turkish empires would be gone within half a decade." Twenty years ago, all those who dismissed Reagan as an "amiable dunce" assured us that the Soviet Union was likewise here to stay. In 1987, there were no experts predicting the imminent fall of the Berlin Wall, the Warsaw pact countries or the USSR itself. All those things happened and supposedly nobody saw it coming. Do you see the clash of civilizations described in this book coming to a mosque near you?

How many times do political leaders and riotous mobs have to chant "Death to America! Death to Israel! And Death to the West!" before our political leaders take notice? Even Newsweek magazine, which certainly was not known for its conservative slant or bias, featured an article by Babak Dehghanpisheh and Christopher Dickey, entitled "The Next Nuclear Threat" in its February 13, 2006 issue.[93] The article stated that Israeli intelligence suggests that a workable Iranian nuclear weapon was less than a decade away. Not since the Ayatollah Khomeini was alive in the 1980s has Iran provoked so many regional and global tensions. "This is the war generation," said Massoud

Denhmaki, a documentary filmmaker in Iran. The survivors of the savage battles between Iraq and Iran in the 1980s have now assumed political power. The younger generation now populating the schools have the attitude that "(A)n Islamic renaissance is starting from here…We are witnessing the start of a fundamentalist uprising in the region from the Muslim Brotherhood in Egypt, to Hamas in Palestine, Hezbollah and Mr. Ahmadinejad in our own country."[94]

Mousa Abu Marzuk, deputy chief of Hamas' political bureau in Damascus, Syria, states that Hamas' political triumph in the Palestinian elections is an important springboard toward the Caliphate, a global Islamic state where life would be dictated by the Sharia.[95]

The spiritual leader of Hamas, the late Ahmad Yassin, once said, "The 21st century is the century of Islam." His successor, Mamood Zahar, stated, "Israel will disappear and after it, the U.S."[96] Obviously, Hamas is not alone. Al Qaeda, Hezbollah and other radical Islamist organizations have openly stated, "We will turn the White House and the British Parliaments into mosques."[97]

And what the radical Islamists cannot achieve by violence, murder, mayhem and terror, they will achieve by political means. They will take advantage of the politically correct, values-neutered West. Sometimes stated as "Stealth Jihad," the global Jihadists of Islam will plant outposts in every nation around the world through their mosques. Once there, they will start the process of feeding as a parasite would on its host until a critical mass is achieved. Then they begin the more serious task of subverting their host by exercising disproportionate influence on the politicians before assuming total control. Like a cancer, Sharia law will insidiously assert itself throughout the culture. For example, a judge in England recently ruled that Sharia law would prevail in certain contract and divorce cases. Tolerance leads to acceptance. Acceptance of the minority culture then leads to subjugation by it as the minority demands ever increasing accommodation and sensitivity. When the majority culture has lost its vision of who it is, it will soon be subsumed by a culture that does have a vision of what it is and where it wants to go. Tolerance is cultural suicide when it's a one-way street. Put another way, tolerance of the intolerant leads to death.

One of Sunni Islam's top clerics, Shiek Yousef al-Qaradhawi, declares on one of his television programs that "Islam will return to Europe as a conqueror and victor." An Imam in Sudan, Mohammed Abd al-Karim preaches that the "Prophet said that the Muslims would take India." The imam who presides over Saudi Arabia's mosque of King Fahd Defense Academy preaches, "We will control the land of the Vatican; we will control Rome and introduce Islam in it. Yes, the Christians, who carved crosses on the breasts of the Muslims in Kosovo and before them in Bosnia, and before them in many places in the world will yet pay us the *jizya* tax in humiliation or they will convert to Islam."[98]

Will Judeo-Christianity survive?

Those familiar with the Book of Revelation already know the answer to this question. In what could be considered the greatest rip-off of Christian writing ever the Muslim Messiah returns to preside over seven years of peace. But, it is not the Twelfth Imam that returns in glory, but the return of Jesus Christ to reign for a thousand years, which prophesy was written first and is found in the Book of Revelation.

What is not divulged in the Book of Revelation is *when* the triumphant return will take place. It is entirely possible that the return may not occur until the world is governed by a Sh'ia caliphate, and with it, intolerance, the degradation of women, the suppression of freedom of speech, freedom of thought, freedom of assembly and freedom of the press. Does this sound like the tribulation? The period of great suffering before Jesus' return? Will the Antichrist of the Book of Revelation arise out of radical Islam?[99] Since the Reformation, the Renaissance, and the Enlightenment, the development of Western political, economic and social thought has birthed societies and countries that have enabled its citizens to enjoy more freedom, more dignity, more prosperity and more advances in science and technology than any civilization in world history.

We in the West and reformist Muslims must therefore denounce the severing of hands and feet as punishment for theft; we must denounce the stoning to death of women as punishment for adultery; and we must continue to strive for equality among all races, religions, colors, and ethnicity. In the short run, we must help reform Islam in the same way that Judaism and Christianity were reformed, through the battle of ideas. But with all the rhetoric and high-mindedness of unity, we as a nation must not forget: When opposed by those who know only the law of the jungle, the law of reason will not prevail. We may have to fight once again for freedom of thought, belief and expression and the sacredness of all human life.

Requiem for a culture

Radical Islamists are militarily weak but ideologically strong. The West is militarily strong but ideologically weak and insecure.

In the end, the real problem facing Western Civilization is *not* how the Muslims might respond to a policy hostile to their interests, but whether the West still has the moral strength to adopt *any* policy short of political correctness.

What legacy will we leave our children?

Will we leave them the light and enlightenment of the Judeo-Christian ethic or a world of radical Muslim darkness for them to stumble through?

A people unwilling to die for their faith or country will die at the hands of a people who are.

Tell your friends and neighbors the threat is real and certain. The alarm bells will have to sound from the bottom up in order for our leaders to take action. Go to the website www.TheUnitedWest.org and get involved! Then pray.

End Notes

Chapter 1

1. Acknowledgement to Norman Podheretz's work "World Ware IV…The Long Struggle Against Islamo Fascism", First Vintage Books, 2008.
2. Washington Post, "Global War on Terror is Given a New Name: by Scott Wilson and Al Kanon, March 25, 2009
3. See Endnote "1"
4. "Berger Will Plead Guilty to Taking Classified Paper", John F. Harris and Allan Lengel, Washington Post, April 1, 2005.
5. "Box cutters found on other September 11 flights", September 24, 2001, CNN.com http://archives.cnn.com/2001/US/09/23/inv.investigation.terrorism/.
6. See also, AmericanCongressforTruth.com, Brigitte Gabriel, Founder.
7. "What Sharia law actually means: The right wants to ban it in America, but do they even know what it is?" by Justin Elliott, February 26, 2011, Salon.com, http://www.salon.com/news/politics/war_room/2011/02/26/sharia_the_real_story
8. See Note 7.
9. See Note 7.
10. See Note 1.
11. Adapted from quotes attributed to Ann Coulter as reported in Associated Press articles appearing in *South Florida Sun-Sentinel,* February, 2006.
12. Tony Blankley, *The West's Last Chance,* Regnery Publishing, Inc., 2005.
13. *Ibid.*

14. *Ibid.*

15. *South Florida Sun-Sentinel,* November 25, 2005.

16. *South Florida Sun-Sentinel,* December 31, 2005.

17. *South Florida Sun Sentinel* January 21, 2008.

18. "Saudi prince changes Fox' Paris riot coverage," by Claire Cozens, December 12, 2005. The UK Guardian quoting Campaign Middle East magazine. http://www.guardian.co.uk/media/2005/dec/12/newscorporation. rupertmurdoch.

19. "Islam film Dutch MP to be charged," June 31, 2009, BBC News, http://news.bbc.co.uk/2/hi/europe/7842344.stm.

20. Bat Ye'or, *Eurabia,* Fairleigh Dickinson University Press, 2005.

21. "Police 'Covered Up' Violent Campaign To Turn London Area 'Islamic,': by Andrew Gilligan, June 16, 2011, the Telegraph. http://www.telegraph.co.UK/news/UKnews/law-and-order/857056/Police-Covered-Up-Violent-Campaign-To-Turn-London-Area-Islamic.html.

22. Foxnews.com, "Violence Creates Terror in Indonesia," Associated Press, December 26, 2005.

23. Found on AmericanCongressforTruth.com, Brigitte Gabriel, Founder.

24. Found on AmericanCongressforTruth.com, Brigitte Gabriel, Founder.

Chapter 2

25. "Barack Obama's speech on Middle East—full transcript", May 19, 2011, reprinted in the Guardian U.K., http://www.guardian .co.uk/world/2011/may/19/barack-obama-speech-middle-east.

26. "Saudi Arabia—End Secrecy, End Suffering: Women's rights," Amnesty International Canada http://www.amenesty.ca.SaudiArabia/5.php.

27. Mark Steyn, *America Alone,* Regnery Publishing, Inc., 2006.

28. Peter Schneider, "The New Berlin Wall, *New York Times Magazine,* December 4, 2005.

29. *Ibid.*

30. Adapted from quotes attributed to Theodore Roosevelt found on TheodoreRoosevelt.com.

31. See Note 2.

32. Such quotes were obtained from websites such as Jihadwatch.com. Such quotes were not figured prominently in the western press.

33. Claire Berlinski, *Menace in Europe,* Crown Publishers, 2006.

34. *Ibid.*

35. *Ibid.*

36. *Ibid.*

Chapter 3

37. First reported at Foxnews.com, "Afghan Man Faces Death for Allegedly Converting to Christianity" Associated Press, March 19, 2006

38. *Ibid..*

39. Serge Trifkovic, *The Sword of the Prophet,* Regina Orthodox Press, 2002

40. *Ibid.*

41. *Ibid.*

42. Robert Spencer, ed., *The Myth of Islamic Tolerance,* Prometheus Books, 2005.

43. David J. Russin, *Take My Wives, Please: Polygamy Heads West*, Pajamas Media, February 29, 2008; http://www.meforum.org/1865/take-my-wives-please-polygamy-heads-west

44. Efraim Karsh, *Islamic Imperialism,* Yale University Press, 2006.

45. See for example, "Muslim-Christian Clashes in Cairo Kill 12, Injure Hundreds." May 8, 2011, Associated Press Report as reported at http://www/foxnews.com/world/2011/05/08/muslim-christian-clashes-kill-10-cairo.

46. See Note 4.

47. See Note 4.

48. See Note 4.

49. Oriana Fallaci, *The Force of Reason,* New York, Rizzoli International Publications, Inc., 2004.

Chapter 4

50. Bernard Goldberg, *Bias,* Regnery Publishing, Inc. 2002.
51. *Ibid.*
52. *Ibid.*
53. As reported by *Investors Business Daily,* November 9, 2007.
54. *Ibid.*
55. *Ibid*
56. *Ibid.*
57. Tim Groseclose, *Left Turn,* St. Martin's Press, New York, 2011.
58. *Ibid.*
59. Alexis de Tocqueville, *Democracy In America,* Gerald Bevan Translator, New York, Penguin Classics, 2003.
60. David Horowitz, *Unholy Alliance,* Washington, D.C. Regnery Publishing Inc., 2004
61. *Ibid*
62. *Ibid.*
63. *Ibid.*
64. *Ibid.*
65. *Ibid.*
66. *Ibid.*
67. Harvey Kushner, *Holy War on the Home Front,* Penguin Group, New York, 2004
68. Harvey Kushner, *Holy War on the Home Front,* Penguin Group, New York, 2004.
69. *Ibid.*
70. *Ibid.*
71. *Ibid.*
72. *Ibid.*
73. See Note 1.
74. *Ibid.*
75. *Ibid.*
76. *Ibid.*

77. *Ibid.*
78. *Ibid.*
79. *Ibid.*
80. *Ibid.*
81. *Ibid.*

Chapter 6

82. Author unknown.
83. Janet L. Folger, *The Criminalization of Christianity*, Sisters Press, Multnomah Publishers, Oregon, 2005.
84. *Ibid.*
85. *Ibid.*
86. *Ibid.*
87. *Ibid.*
88. Remarks delivered by U.S. Senator Rick Santorum at the National Press Club, July 20, 2006.
89. Kenneth R. Timmerman, *Countdown to Crisis* , Three Rivers Press, New York, 2005.
90. Adapted from a website known as, republicworldnews.com.
91. Adapted from "December 7, 2008," by Raymond S. Kraft, appearing on www.youdontsay.org, October 24, 2006.
92. *Newsweek,* February 13, 2006.
93. *Ibid.*
94. Rachel Ehrenfeld, "The Caliphate is Coming," FrontPagemagazine.com, January 31, 2006.
95. *Ibid.*
96. *Ibid.*
97. *Ibid.*
98. *Ibid*

About the Author

A distinguished trial attorney in Florida for 30 years, Peter Feaman owns his own firm and was appointed to the 15th Judicial Circuit Nominating Commission and the Fourth District Court of Appeal Nominating Commission. He is also a member of the Republican Party of Florida and serves on its Executive Committee. He has published articles and editorials in the *Boca Raton News and Sun-Sentinel*. Feaman's law background factors heavily into his motivation to write about the Islamist movement. Mr. Feaman is the author of *Wake Up, America!* and he resides in Boca Raton, Florida.